Jordan

and Sinai
A handbook for Christian
visitors

John Hayden

Honey Hill Publishing
St Mary's Church, Honey Hill, Bury St Edmunds, Suffolk IP33 1RT, UK

© 2010 John Hayden and Honey Hill Publishing

First published in 2000 by Honey Hill Publishing
This edition, revised and expanded, first published in 2010

Quotations from the Bible are taken from the New International Version (USA edition) and are used by permission of the copyright holders, the International Bible Society, Colorado Springs, USA.

ISBN 978-0-9554504-2-6

Honey Hill Publishing is an enterprise of St Mary's Church, Bury St Edmunds, Suffolk, UK.

Index

Introduction

Visiting the Middle East today plunges a Christian back into the world of the Bible. Sites within the present countries of Palestine and Israel may be the most familiar but the surrounding countries have much to offer. Not only do they have some of the most spectacular sites but most of these are unspoiled and give one a real feel for what it was like before modern-day development took over.

The purpose of this book is not to provide the kind of guided tour given by the local guides, nor is it to replace information that can easily be obtained in the published guide books. In that regard the *Footprint* series is by far the best one-volume series available.

In the Bible, Jordan features as the area through which Moses under God led the Israelites to the Promised Land. One of the best ways to experience this is to begin in Egypt and follow that journey. Some may not be able to do this but I hope that reading the account of this journey through Sinai to Nebo will help bring to life whatever section of it you follow personally.

This handbook contains:

A Key facts on each place as it appears in the biblical narrative. Visits will obviously include many other places but these are selected because of their Christian significance.

B All the biblical references to those sites. In this section, with kind permission of the International Bible Society, I have listed all the biblical references to the places covered in Section A. All quotations need to be read in the context in which they are found within the Bible. Such an exercise will be amply rewarded. In Section A I have started this study by drawing attention to some of these references. As the Bible is not in date order when listed below, I have given a rough guide to the times to which passages relate.

Finally, I am deeply indebted to Lance Bidewell for the considerable task he has undertaken in editing this handbook.

Bishop John Haydcn   January 2010

Some useful guidelines

It is worth remembering that Israel was, and for that matter still is, hostile to the surrounding nations. Many of the passages need to be read in the context of God's judgment on those who oppose his plans, and not as God's condemnation on the present-day peoples of those countries.

Historical events need to be read in the light of the standards of their day. We live in an age when most countries have signed the UN Charter of Human Rights and so can be judged by the way those rights, such as freedom of religion, are maintained. In the days of Moses the maxim 'an eye for an eye and a tooth for a tooth applied to all rich or poor alike' was seen as a major step away from the unjust revenge of the day. In the same way we need to judge the Persian, Greek, Roman, Muslim and Crusader invasions of the countries. No age and no person is without fault. The key point is to learn from the past rather than judge it from today's standards.

I have tried to avoid the use of abbreviations but it is worth noting that a lower case 'c.' stands for the Latin '*circa*' meaning 'about.'

In Egypt

Genesis ends with the family of Israel settled in Egypt. Four hundred years later that family had grown into a nation within a nation. They began to dominate the north-east of Egypt. The most likely route for any invasion of the country was from that corner and Pharaoh feared they might join the enemy. So he forced them into building supply cities for his army. He also tried to introduce a policy of infanticide.

Moses was born of Hebrew parents and during her time of guardianship his mother taught him about his origins and his God. As a young man Moses left her care to live in the court and seems to have been trained alongside the other princes.

At around the age of forty he felt that God had chosen him to free his people from their slavery. Unfortunately he had gone a step ahead of God and was forced to flee to Midian. The Midianites who lived on the Sinai peninsula were distant relatives (Genesis 25:2ff). Moses lived for many years in the tents of Jethro, one of their chiefs whose daughter Zipporah he had married. The region was semi-desert and was firstrate training in desert life and their tribal customs.

In the meantime his people continued to suffer. The time for their deliverance was at hand and God came to Moses while he was 'tending the flock of Jethro' (Exodus 2:1). Was it the appearance of God in the burning bush that later led Moses to return to that holy place with the whole nation of Israel? God revealed himself to Moses as יהוה . Hebrew was written with consonants only so we can only guess the vowels. The most likely ones make the word Yahweh, which means 'I am'.

God sends Moses and his brother Aaron to seek from Pharaoh the release of his people. Pharaoh refuses and there follow the nine plagues. God uses the physical characteristics of the Nile valley to produce them. The first plague polluted the water, the fish died and so forced the frogs out of the water. Gnats and flies were to follow, and from them came a plague of cattle disease followed by an outbreak of skin disease among the Egyptians. All through the plagues Pharaoh was given an opportunity to repent. He did not and God sent a plague of hail, followed by locusts which ate up what remained of the damaged crops. Frightening darkness descended and still Pharaoh refused to let the people go. So the history leads on to the dreadful plague of the first-born. God was going to use this last plague to teach the people of Israel that their protection depended on him alone. Each family would only be delivered by killing a sacrificial animal as a substitute and sprinkling the lamb's blood on the doorpost of their home. The Passover feast had to be prepared quickly for the people must be ready to leave next morning.

The terror-stricken Egyptians now urged the instant departure of the Hebrews. In the midst of the Passover feast, before the dawn of the fifteenth day of the month Abib (our April), which was to be to them the beginning of the year, as it was the start of a new epoch in their history, every family, with all that they had, was ready for the march, which instantly began under the leadership of the heads of tribes with their various subdivisions. They moved onward, increasing as they went forward from all the districts of Goshen and elsewhere. It may have taken three or four days before they were assembled at Rameses, and ready to set out under their leader Moses (Exodus 12:37; Numbers 33:3). This city was at that time the residence of the Egyptian court, and it was here that the interviews between Moses and Pharaoh took place.

They were poor; for generations they had laboured for the Egyptians without wages. They asked gifts from their neighbours around them (Exodus 12:35), and these were readily given. One day those gifts were to be used to construct the tabernacle for the worship of God!

We would expect that the Israelites, having seen the result of God's judgment on the Egyptians, would carry with them the indelible impression of God's power and holiness. Sadly it was not to be.

In I Corinthians 10:1-5 Paul sums up their history as a warning to us:
> For I do not want you to be ignorant of the fact, brothers, that our forefathers were all under the cloud and that they all passed through the sea. They were all baptized into Moses in the cloud and in the sea. They all ate the same spiritual food and drank the same spiritual drink; for they drank from the spiritual rock that accompanied them, and that rock was Christ. Nevertheless, God was not pleased with most of them; their bodies were scattered over the desert.

The Pyramids of Giza

The great pyramid of Giza is perhaps the largest building ever constructed. Close by are two smaller pyramids and together they were classed as one of the seven wonders of the world. Also nearby are the remains of temples and smaller pyramids and flat-topped tombs.

The great pyramid was built for King Khufu, or Cheops. It was built between 2600 and 2500 BC. Herodotus, writing 2,000 years later, claims that it took twenty years to build and that 100,000 men were constantly employed in shifts to transport the stones from the east bank of the Nile and bring them to the site on huge rafts. (All pyramids are on the west bank, the side of the setting sun.) The builders used 2,300,000 blocks of limestone or granite, each weighing about 2.5 tons. At the time the pulley and wheels were not invented so the physical exertion was phenomenal. It is 230.4 metres square at the base but its peak is only 10 centimetres square. It is 145.7 metres high. Originally the sides were covered with a light limestone and were smooth but this coating has been lost, leaving the granite steps.

On the north facing wall is the only door. The passageway leads to the Queen's Chamber; a Grand Hall, 46 metres long; an unfinished room; and then the vast pink granite King's Chamber. Here the King's mummified body was put to rest within a sarcophagus carved from a single stone. Originally the room would have been filled with the belongings that his spirit needed in the afterlife, but ancient Egyptian robbers, with no respect for the dead, and defying the curse laid on anyone who opened the door, were in the habit of robbing all tombs, including the pyramids. After the king was buried, all the passageways were filled and sealed and the door hidden

Next to the great pyramid is that of Pharaoh Chephren. It is slightly shorter. Everything has been removed except the Pharaoh's granite coffin. The third pyramid of Mycerinus had a carved basalt coffin but it was lost off the coast of Spain with the ship that was bringing it to England in the reign of Queen Victoria!

The Sphinx has recently been renovated. It was carved from a single rock into the likeness of Chephren but with a lion's body. Over the centuries the sand that blows in from the desert has had to be cleared away.   An inscription placed between its paws tells of one such time in the fifteenth century BC.   A prince out hunting rested in its shade and dreamed that if he removed the sand he would receive the double crown of Egypt.   He did so and succeeded to the throne.

Life and death

The sun dies each evening and then rises again, so it was believed that the pharaoh, an embodiment of the sun, must also have an afterlife and at death rejoin his divine father in the sky.   At death the soul flew away like a bird.   There seemed to be no idea of the resurrection of the body, yet at death it was mummified and buried with things that would be needed in the afterlife.   The Egyptians appeared to believe there could be a spiritual counterpart in the world beyond for any object in this life.   So they sought to project into that world the good things they had enjoyed in this life.   As the Pharaoh was the embodiment of the gods and in some sense god incarnate, the plagues of the exodus were a direct attack on the gods themselves.   They worshipped the Nile as the god Hapi, yet God turned it into blood that stank.   They worshipped the sun as Amon-Re or Ra, yet God brought intense darkness over the land.

The Egyptian Museum

The collection includes over 120,000 items. The museum opened in 1858 and was moved to its present site in 1902. There are over one hundred halls so any visit is very selective. Of major interest to the Christian pilgrim are the exhibits from the Middle Kingdom (Patriarchs) and the New Kingdom (Moses). Most tours include the ground floor rooms 48,47,46,42,32, covering the Old Kingdom, rooms 11 & 12 (New Kingdom) and the Tutankhamen exhibit.

The Museum is divided into the following sections:
1   Tutankhamen's treasures.
2   Pre-dynasty and the Old Kingdom monuments.
3   Intermediate and Middle Kingdom.
4   The Modern Kingdom.
5   Late and the Greek and Roman periods.
6   Coins and papyri.
7   Sarcophagi and scrabs.
8   Royal mummies - housing eleven kings and queens.

Plan of rooms – the numbers are virtually the same on both floors.

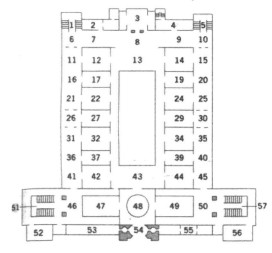

Tutankhamen ruled from 1333 BC to 1324 BC, so this was around the time of Moses. The 1,700 pieces on display give us a good impression of life in an era when Israel was taking shape as an independent nation.

St Mary's Church, Old Cairo

This church, dedicated to the Virgin Mary, is probably the most famous Coptic church in Cairo. It is popularly know as the Suspended or Hanging Church, from its Arabic name al-Muallaqah. The name derives from it being built over a passageway above the gate of the old Roman fortress. In earlier times it really did appear suspended but the street level has risen six metres. Even so it is approached by a flight of 29 steps.

There was a church on this site from the fourth century but most of the present building dates from the seventh and tenth centuries. There is a nineteenth century facade with twin bell towers and the entrance courtyard is decorated with modern biblical mosaics.

By the eleventh century, the Hanging Church became the official residence of the Coptic patriarchs of Alexandria and several Coptic synods were held in the church.

If time allows it is still possible to visit the Roman remains below the present church but there is plenty to see without this. On entering it is good to look up at the wooden roof. The beams are similar to an upturned boat and give the impression of Noah's ark.

There are well over 100 icons in the church dating back to the eighth century. Recently some of these have been restored to their former vibrant colours.

The Iconostasis (sanctuary screen) dates from the twelfth or thirteenth century. It is made of ebony inlaid with ivory, carved with geometric designs and Coptic crosses, and has above it a row of seven large icons. The centre icon depicts the Pantocrator, Christ Enthroned; to his left are John the Baptist, the Archangel Michael and St Paul; to his right are the Virgin Mary, the Archangel Gabriel and St Peter.

To the left of this central iconostasis is a another screen of ebony and ivory. Its 17 icons depict the martyrdom of St George. Across the top of the right screen are seven icons depicting the life of St John the Baptist. All the icons on these screens are the work of an eighteenth century Armenian artist, Orhan Karabedian.

The 11th-century marble pulpit surmounts 13 fine pillars, representing Jesus and the 12 disciples. As customary in Coptic churches, one of the pillars is black, representing Judas, and another is grey, for doubting Thomas. Its steps are carved with a shell and a cross.

After a recent restoration many objects that were no longer in regular use or of major historical value are now in the Coptic Museum. These include a lintel showing Christ's entry into Jerusalem which dates from the fifth or sixth century.

Plan of Old Cairo Christian quarter

Ben Ezra Synagogue

The synagogue was originally the fourth to sixth century church of St Michael. It was sold to the Jews in AD 882 to pay for the taxes imposed on the Christians by the Muslim rulers. Ben Ezra bought the property for 20,000 dinars or 'kanters of gold'.

Many restorations have taken place and most of today's building dates from 1892. At this time a Geniza, or hiding place, for sacred books and scrolls was discovered. Found hidden were thousands of documents dating from the Fatimid era. They were first written in Aramaic and later in Hebrew Arabic. 'Hebrew Arabic' is a variation of Arabic in Hebrew alphabet, exclusively used by Jews in the Middle Ages, which reflected political, economic and social conditions of Jews under the Arab rule of Egypt as well as sectarian organizations and relations between different Jewish sects. This collection, known as the Cairo Geniza, is now housed at Cambridge University where it was brought by Solomon Schechter. The GOLD (Genizah On-Line Database) contains over 1,200 manuscript images. There are a number of rare commentaries on the Hebrew scriptures and ones dealing with Jewish/Muslim relationships.

The synagogue was a place of pilgrimage for North African Jews and the site of major festival celebrations. The famous medieval rabbi Moses Maimonides worshipped at Ben Ezra synagogue when he lived in Cairo. When nearly all the Jews left Egypt in 1956 and 1967 it was left to decay along with Cairo's other 25 synagogues. In the 1990s with the help of an American donor and the Egyptian government, the synagogue was restored to its former glory and a Jewish heritage library was opened in November 1997.

At the back of the synagogue is an ancient well where it is said that the 'ark' made by Moses' mother to hide him from the Egyptians was found. The Jews also claim it to be the site where Jeremiah preached and was later buried. Another legend is that this is the place where Mary bathed Jesus.

The synagogue is based on the Christian basilica style with two floors, the lower floor being for men and the upper one for women. However, no services take place as there are not enough Jews left to employ a rabbi. The floor is divided into three areas and in the centre is an octagonal marble bima (a platform from which the Torah is read).

St Sergius and St Bacchus

The Roman fort area of Cairo known as Babylon is entered through two huge towers. In this area is the Church of St Sergius and St Bacchus, known locally as Abu Serga. Sergius and Bacchus were soldiers who were martyred in Syria in the fourth century under the Emperor Maximilian.

It was founded in the fourth century in an area where it is claimed that the Holy Family lived during their time in Egypt. It is also claimed that Joseph found work at the fortress. That seems unlikely, as it was the Roman fort rather than the Jewish area and the major community of Jews lived in Alexandria, not Cairo. The crypt where the Holy Family may have lived is the sanctuary of the original church and is about six metres square. It is 10 metres below ground level and is often flooded by the Nile waters.

The church is of the early Byzantine type. It was burnt down and rebuilt in the eighth century and has undergone restoration several times since then. The building is rectangular with a nave and two side aisles. The roof beams are exposed and it has galleries each side over the aisles. Men usually sit in the central aisle and women in the side aisles. The main nave columns are of interest as they seem to have come from various ancient buildings and so are of an irregular colour and size. One is of red granite and the other eleven are marble. Faint paintings are still visible on them but are too indistinct to make out who they depict.

The church is entered by the south-west corner, although it was originally entered in the west where the narthex, divided by wooden screens, still exists. The central area of the narthex was used for the foot-washing ceremony of the Epiphany and in the north area is the font. Those awaiting baptism would worship in the narthex.

Like the church of St Mary, the iconostasis is ebony inlaid with ivory and probably dates from the twelfth century. There are some even older icons, painted on wood, depicting Sergius and Bacchus on horseback, the Nativity and the Last Supper. Other icons dating from the seventeenth century depict scenes from the life of Christ and some of the lives of the saints. This church often rivalled the Church of St Mary and claims it was the place where many of the patriarchs were elected and were consecrated until the eleventh century.

St Barbara's Church

This church was originally dedicated to St Cyrus and St John, but when the remains of St Barbara were brought here a separate sanctuary was built, making it a church with two sanctuaries. Because of the fame of St Barbara the church soon assumed that name.

St Barbara lived in the third century and was the daughter of a wealthy merchant in Heliopolis. He discovered that his daughter had become a Christian and was refusing to marry the man he had chosen for her, so he asked the Roman Governor Marcianus to torture her until she denied Christ. After the first day of torture she was standing in a pool of her own blood but during the night she was healed. The next day she still refused to recant and her father killed her with his own sword, along with her servant, Juliana. Her remains were brought to this church in the eleventh century.

The original church could date back to the fourth century but was considerably enlarged by a wealthy secretary, Athanasius, in the seventh century. There have been several adaptations and restorations, including one around a hundred years ago. The church is now below street level.

Architecturally it is very similar to that of the church of St Sergius and St Bacchus and has a narthex, nave with side aisles and three sanctuaries – the central one dedicated to St Barbara. Her remains are in a chapel of the church.

It has a number of icons but its main treasures are in the nearby Coptic Museum. The most interesting of such finds is a door made of sycamore wood dating from the fifth century. Of special note are icons from the thirteenth century depicting Christ surrounded by angels.

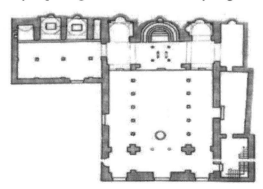

Saints

The Coptic Church has a full calendar of commemorations for the saints. There are those who are on the church's worldwide calendar, like the apostles, but there are also local saints. Such details are available on the Coptic Church official website and pilgrims might like to look these up to link with a visit to Egypt. An example of this information is that of two saints who are commemorated on 11 April.

1. The Departure of St John, Bishop of Jerusalem.

> On this day Anba John, Bishop of Jerusalem, departed. He was born to Jewish parents, who kept the Law of the Torah. They instructed and taught him well and he excelled in the Law of Moses. He argued and disputed with the Christians until he became convinced of the coming of the Lord Christ, and that He was the true God. He believed on the hand of St Justus, Bishop of Jerusalem, who baptized and ordained him a deacon. Because of his knowledge and virtues they chose him a bishop of Jerusalem after the departure of St Justus.

> When Andrianus reigned, he commanded to rebuild the ruined parts of the city, he built a tower on the western gate (the gate of the Jewish temple) and he hanged an engraved tablet with his name on the door of that gate. He prevented the Christians from praying at the Golgotha and even passing through it. The Jews and the Gentiles became powerful and troubled the Christians much. Because of that many tribulations and sorrows befell this father, so he asked God that He might receive him. His supplication was accepted and he departed in peace after he stayed on the Episcopal Chair for two years.

2. The Departure of the holy father Anba Michael, the seventy-first Pope of the See of St Mark.

On this day also of the year 862 A.M. (March 29th. 1146 A.D.) the holy father Pope Michael, the seventy first Patriarch of the See of St Mark, departed. He longed for the pure life since his young age so he became a monk in the monastery of St Macarius. He lived in the desert until he was an old man, in a good pleasing life to God.

When Pope Gabriel (70) departed, the bishops, the priests and the lay leaders spent three months searching for who was best suited to succeed him. A monk from the monastery of St Macarius, called Yoannis Ebn Kedran, came forward nominating himself supported in that by Anba Yacoub, bishop of Lekanah, Anba Christodolus, bishop of Fowa, and Anba Michael, bishop of Tanta.

Nevertheless, the bishops of Upper Egypt, the priests of Alexandria and the lay leaders of Cairo did not accept that choice. Finally they all agreed to choose three of the monks and those were: Yoannis Abu El-Fatah, Michael of St Macarius monastery, and Soliman El-Dekhiary of El-Baramous monastery. They cast a lot among them, and the lot fell on the monk Michael, and they ordained him a Patriarch on the 5th of Mesra, 861 A.M. (July 29th, year 1145 A.D.). He was an honourable old man loving for the poor and the needy. He took for himself a scribe to write his sermons and teachings that he sent to the bishops and priests. When he fell sick, he went to the monastery of St. Macarius, where he departed in peace, after he stayed on the Chair for eight months.

St Mark's Cathedral

St Mark's Coptic Orthodox Cathedral is located in the Abbassia District in Cairo, Egypt. It is the current seat of the Coptic Orthodox Pope. It was built during the time when Pope Cyril VI of Alexandria was Pope of the Coptic Orthodox Church and inaugurated by Pope Cyril in 1968.

The Cathedral is built on land that was a Coptic cemetery from 969. Soon ten churches were built on the site but were destroyed in 1280 by Qalawan. They were later replaced by two churches. The Copts were in danger of losing the land in 1943 but after a lengthy case were allowed to keep the land if a non-profit making building was erected on it.

The architecture is an interesting blend of the old and new styles.

Before the completion of the Cathedral in 1968, Pope Paul VI returned part of St Mark's relics, which were stolen from Egypt in the year 828 and removed to Venice, Italy. These relics were taken to the newly constructed Cathedral, where they were placed in a specially built shrine brightly decorated with Coptic icons.

The Coptic Cathedral of St Mark is by far the largest cathedral in Africa. It is the seat of the current Coptic Pope, His Holiness Pope Shenouda III, Pope and Patriarch of Alexandria and the See of St Mark.

Note: The Basilica of Our Lady of Peace of Yamoussoukro in Yamoussoukro, Côte d'Ivoire, the largest church in the world, is not a cathedral. The nearby Cathedral of Saint Augustine is the principal place of worship and seat of the Bishop of the Diocese of Yamoussoukro.

Athanasius

Athanasius was born in Alexandria sometime between AD 293 and 300 and died there in 373. He attended the Council of Nicaea in 325 as the key advisor to Bishop Alexander of Alexandria and was the main force behind the adoption of the Nicene Creed. Arius, also from Alexandria, had argued that the Son of God was not eternal but created by the Father. He was not God by nature. Athanasius saved the Christian church by insisting that the Son of God was *homoousios*: consubstantial, co-eternal and co-equal. When Alexander died three years after Nicaea, Alexander became bishop (patriarch) until his death forty-five years later. Seventeen of those years were spent in exile as he strongly defended, against the emperors, the truth as expressed in the Nicaean Creed.

Athanasius was a prolific writer. He wrote against the Arians, various defences of the Christian faith like the *Incarnation of the Word*, Easter messages (the one for AD 367 sets out for the first time the list of New Testament books as we have them today) and the *Life of Anthony,* whom Athanasius regarded as the first monk.

Athanasius fought so hard for the deity of Christ because he realized that He alone could save us. He argued his case from the Bible and from worship – if Jesus is not God then we should not worship Him. Only the one through whom the world was created could restore it. Such restoration could only be by an act of God: in this case on the cross. This highlights the difference between western and eastern thought. Western thought concentrates on the removal of the guilt of sin that separates us from God. Eastern thought concentrates on a restoration of man into the image of God. In the incarnation human and divine natures are reunited. 'He became what we are that he might make us what he is'. (*Incarnation of the Word*)

Below is a quotation from the *Incarnation of the Word*, in which Athanasius brings together western and eastern concepts and is a reason why he appealed to both sides of the divide.

We were the cause of his becoming flesh. For our salvation he loved us so much as to appear and be born in a human body.... No one else but the Saviour himself, who in the beginning made everything out of nothing, could bring the corruptible to incorruptible; no one else but the image of the Father could recreate men in God's image; no one else but our Lord Jesus Christ, who is Life itself, could make the mortal immortal; no one else but the Word, who orders everything and is alone the true and only begotten Son of the Father, could teach men about the Father and destroy idolatry. Since the debt owed by all men had to be paid he came among us. After he had demonstrated his deity by his works, he offered his sacrifice on behalf of all and surrendered his temple (body) to death in the place of all men. He did this to free men from the guilt of the first sin and to prove himself more powerful than death, showing his own body incorruptible, as a first-fruit of the resurrection of all ... He endured men's insults that we might inherit immortality.

Some other quotes:

For the Word was not degraded by receiving a body; rather he deified what he put on.

The Word of God was not made for us, rather we were made for him.

Mankind had lost the knowledge of God and the image of God in which he was made. How could he be restored? Only by God's Word.

For this reason he was born, appeared as man, and died and rose again... that, wherever men may have been lured away, he may recall them from there, and reveal to them his own true Father; as he himself says, 'I came to seek and to save what was lost'.

I think the Psalms are like a mirror, in which one can see oneself and the movements of one's own heart.

Monasticism

The appeal of denying oneself bodily needs in order to concentrate on spiritual matters is common to humanity. In the early Christian church this way of life flourished in Egypt.

Our information about St Anthony comes from a biography written by Athanasius. Anthony began his monastic pilgrimage by living in a tomb some distance from his village. A friend brought him food from time to time. Then he moved into the remote mountains and found an abandoned fort in which he made his home. A stream provided him with water and friends brought him some food twice a year. He lived in total isolation without seeing anyone for twenty years, in constant battle with 'demons'.

At the age of fifty-five he offered himself as a teacher to others who wished to follow his example. Before long the remote desert hills of Egypt were populated by his followers. He and his followers were arrested under Maximilian's persecution but on arrival in Alexandria the officials ordered them straight out of the city and back into the desert. Anthony and his followers returned to their desert dwelling in early 312 but not to the peace and solitude he had known. Fame became unbearable so he wandered off again and this time found a place where he could feed himself and be in perfect solitude. He died over a 100 years old in AD 356.

Athanasius comments that Anthony's increasingly severe acts of self-denial led him into a thousand forms of physical torment. It was his victory over these which enabled him to become a model ascetic. God blessed him with visions, foreknowledge and miraculous healing.

Athanasius records a long sermon which he attributes to Anthony, where he claims that the whole life of an ascetic should be dominated by the Last Judgment and each day was to be lived as if it was their last. The 'path of virtue' was one of wisdom, uprightness, temperance, courage and insight. Christian love, meekness, hospitality and, above all, faith in Christ should dominate.. However, Athanasius makes it clear that this way of life is very much open to the criticism that it is self-justification and in it Christ is only an example. The ascetic – the word comes from the Greek word *askein',* used of an athlete's training schedule – has through his own life overcome the demons that surround him.

The followers of Anthony were living out Matthew 19:21 'If you would be perfect, go sell what you possess and give to the poor ... And come follow me.' Their asceticism included abstinence from certain kinds of food and drink, all forms of enjoyment and human support like marriage and ordinary comforts of life. These were replaced by set times of prayer and devotions. Each one lived alone, meditated, prayed and worshipped alone.

Another form of monasticism arose. Its leader was Pachomius, a former soldier under Constantine. He began his spiritual journey living under the rule of Anthony but soon realized there was a place for community. His followers came together in large settlements often numbering many hundreds. Their day was highly regulated, with times set apart for prayer but also for physical work to provide their own food and water. Work was considered necessary not only to live but to be human.

There is no doubt that Athanasius played a major part in the growth of monasticism throughout the Christian world. He was an Egyptian, as were Anthony and Pachomius who were his friends whom he visited out in the desert. In his travels, sometimes enforced by exile to countries like France, he spread the message that he wrote in his *Life of Anthony.*

Fasting is one of the many legacies of the Monastic tradition in the Coptic Church. The Copts have more seasons of fasting than Christians from any other tradition. Out of the 365 days of the year, Copts fast for over 210 days. During fasting, no animal products (meat, poultry, fish, milk, eggs, butter, etc.) are allowed. On a more strict level, no food or drink whatsoever may be taken between sunrise and sunset, as they should only break their fast after Communion.

Fasting seasons of the Coptic Church include the Fast of the Nativity ('Christmas') which is 45 days, the Fast of the Apostles, the Fast of the Virgin Mary, the Fast of Nineveh, and of course Lent, known as The Great Fast and which lasts 55 days. Other than the fasting holidays, many Copts also fast on Wednesdays and Fridays all year.

Monastery of St Anthony

The fortress-like Coptic monastery of St Anthony the Great stands at an oasis spring in the Red Sea Mountains, at the foot of Mount Al-Qalzam. It was founded in AD 356, on Saint Anthony's burial site. It is the oldest Christian monastery in the world.

In the sixth and seventh centuries many monks from the Natroun valley north of Cairo moved here to escape persecution. The monastery was frequently plundered by Bedouin, and to provide protection, strong walls were built that today give it a fortress-like appearance.

The monks who live here still speak Coptic, a language directly descended from the language of the ancient Egyptians.

It is a self-contained centre with gardens, a mill, a bakery and five churches. The Church of St Anthony is a major treasure. Some of its wall paintings date from the sixth and the ninth centuries, and among them is a picture of the founder, St Anthony himself. They have recently been restored, removing the dirt and grease of many centuries, and now reveal their vibrant colours. There is also some fine wood carving.

A library of 1,700 handwritten manuscripts is all that remains of a much larger library plundered by the Bedouin and used as cooking fuel.

The cave of St Antony is a two kilometre climb up the mountain.

St Paul's Monastery

St Paul of Thebes began his life of solitude in the desert several years before St Anthony, who visited him on his deathbed and buried the saint nearby. Jerome claims that Paul of Thebes was the first hermit and that Anthony was his pupil.

The monastery, built on the grave of St Paul, dates from sometime in the fifth century. Like St Anthony's, it was often plundered and so many precious items have been lost. Over the centuries it was occupied by Melkites and Syrians as well as Egyptians. Today it is a branch of the St Anthony's monastery.

The monastery has three churches. The Church of St Paul, built underground, was dug into the cave where the saint lived and where his remains are kept.

St Paul's monastery possesses many illustrated manuscripts, including the Coptic version of the Divine Liturgy and the Commentary on the Epistle of Saint Paul to Titus by John Chrysostom.

The two other churches are named after Saint Mercurius and the Archangel Michael. The monastery is surrounded by high walls, built during the eighteenth and nineteenth centuries. It also has a tower (keep), an ancient refectory, a mill, and a spring that is believed to have served Saint Paul the Anchorite during his eighty years of seclusion in this area. A second spring, known as the Pool of Mary, is named after Mary (Miriam) the sister of Moses, who is believed to have washed her feet there during the Exodus.

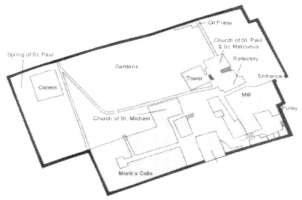

The Exodus

There is a lack of evidence for the exact route taken by the Israelites when they fled Egypt. Some suggest a route that crosses the reed sea or area of swamp land that now forms the route of the Suez canal in the north; some opt for a crossing in the centre; some in the south. We will choose the southern route for three reasons: it is likely to be the one used by Moses on his journeys to his father-in-law and passes through an area he had known for the last forty years; it avoids the line of Egyptian fortresses further north; it fits in with the description of the journey that we have in the Bible.

The Israelites left Rameses on the Nile Delta and reached Succoth (Exodus 12:37), identified with Tel-el-Maskhuta, about 12 miles west of Ismailia. Their next camp, Etham, was probably close to the modern town of Ismailia, on the Suez Canal (Exodus 13:20). Here they were commanded 'to turn and encamp before Pi-hahiroth, between Migdol and the sea', i.e., to change their route from east to due south. God now led the direction of their march with the pillar of cloud by day and of fire by night along the shore of the 'Yam Suph' (sea of reeds) until they reached Pi-hahioth, about 40 miles from Etham. The exact spot of their camp before they crossed the 'Yam Suph' cannot be determined. It was probably somewhere near the present site of Suez.

God led the people on through the 'Yam Suph', the wind clearing a dry route for them to cross on foot. The Egyptians, riding in chariots, found the route blocked by mud and water and were unable to follow. The whole military force of the Egyptians perished. As Miriam's song puts it, they 'sank to the depths like a stone' (Exodus 15:5). Having reached the eastern shore of the sea, perhaps a little way to the north of 'Ayun Musa' (the springs of Moses), there they camped and rested, probably for a day.

> Then Moses led Israel from the Red Sea and they went into the Desert of Shur. For three days they travelled in the desert without finding water. When they came to Marah ('bitter'), they could not drink its water because it was bitter. So the people grumbled against Moses, saying, 'What are we to drink?' Then Moses cried out to the Lord, and the Lord showed him a piece of wood. He threw it into the water, and the water became sweet. (Exodus 15:22ff)

Later they came to Elim, where there were twelve springs and seventy palm trees, and they camped there near the water.

They then camped by the Red Sea (Numbers 33:10), and moved on to the Sin Desert (Exodus 16:1) Here, probably the modern el-Markha, the supplies of food they had brought with them out of Egypt failed. They began to grumble, but God heard and gave them quails and manna (manna means 'What is it?'), 'bread from heaven' (Exodus 16:4-36). Moses directed that an omer of manna should be put aside and preserved as a perpetual memorial of God's goodness.

They now turned inland, and after three encampments came to the rich and fertile valley of Rephidim, in the Wadi Feiran. Here they found no water, and again murmured against Moses. Directed by God, Moses procured a miraculous supply of water from the 'rock in Horeb', one of the hills of the Sinai group (Exodus 17:1-7); and shortly afterwards the children of Israel here fought their first battle with the Amalekites, whom they defeated. The line of march now probably led through the Wadi esh-Sheikh and the Wadi Solaf, meeting in the Wadi er-Rahah, 'the enclosed plain in front of the magnificent cliffs of Ras Sufsafeh'. Here at Sinai they encamped for more than a year (Numbers 1:1).

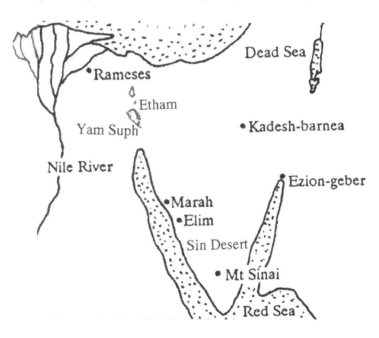

Sinai

Since the fourth century AD Mount Sinai has been located in the southern part of the Sinai peninsula. The present monastery of St Catherine, on the north-west slope of Jebel Musa (7,500ft) was founded in AD 527 on the site of a small church built two centuries earlier. Jebel Musa is one of three summits: Ras-es-Safsaf to the north-west, Jebel Musa to the south-east and Jebel Katarin (8,500ft) to the south-west. The mountain is sometimes called Horeb, meaning desolate region, but where both names occur together Horeb is the area and Sinai the mountain.

From Rephidim (Exodus 17:8-13) the Israelites journeyed forward through the Wadi Solaf and Wadi esh-Sheikh into the plain of er-Rahah, 'the desert of Sinai', about two miles long and half a mile broad, and camped there 'before the mountain'. Dean Stanley thus describes the scene:

> The plain itself is not broken and uneven and narrowly shut in, like almost all others in the range, but presents a long retiring sweep, within which the people could remove and stand afar off. The cliff, rising like a huge altar in front of the whole congregation, and visible against the sky in lonely grandeur from end to end of the whole plain, is the very image of the 'mount that might be touched,' and from which the voice of God might be heard far and wide over the plain below.

This was the scene of the giving of the law. The last twenty-two chapters of Exodus, together with the whole of Leviticus and Numbers 1-11, contain a record of the covenant and transactions which occurred while they were here.

Before receiving the detailed requirements of the covenant, the people were given a brief view of the power and holiness of God. A boundary was drawn round the mountain to keep them at a distance. For two days they had to carry out symbolic acts of cleansing before they were allowed to look towards Mount Sinai. On the third day there was a great storm on the mountain – thick cloud with thunder and lightning, and on top of that an earthquake. God then spoke to Moses on the top of the mountain (Exodus 19).

The Decalogue (ten words or commands) follows a pattern common in the ancient world. God, the overlord, introduces himself and recounts what he has done for them. The ten commands that follow are basic principles by which the nation should live and on which the detailed laws of the nation would be based. The first three commands concern their attitude to God. The Sabbath command provides a time for the people to worship God, and a time for the people to rest. The six final commands deal with personal duties.

These basic principles of Exodus 20 are followed by a series of 'case laws' that set the standard by which the principles are to be kept. They fit in with the society that already existed and bring it toward the standard laid down by God. There are key differences from the tribal law codes of the day. In the 'law of Moses' the punishment had to fit the crime. It was the same for everyone, regardless of status, and all had to be given a fair hearing. So it protected the defenceless and disadvantaged.

So from Sinai the law was proclaimed to the people camped below in the plain of er-Rahah. During the lengthened period of their stay here the Israelites passed through a very memorable experience. An immense change passed over them. They were now an organized nation, bound by covenant engagement to serve the Lord their God, their ever-present divine leader and protector.

At length, in the second month of the second year of the Exodus, they moved their camp and marched forward according to a prescribed order. After three days they reached the 'wilderness of Paran', the 'et-Tih', i.e., 'the desert', and here they made their first stop. At this time a spirit of discontent broke out amongst them, and the Lord showed his displeasure by a fire which fell on the camp and inflicted injury on them. Moses called the place Taberah (Numbers 11:1-3). The journey between Sinai and the southern boundary of the Promised Land (about 150 miles) at Kadesh was accomplished in about a year.

In the time of King Ahab (ninth century BC) Elijah made a pilgrimage to the holy mountain (1 Kings 19). God spoke to him there. Elijah had expected to find God, as Moses had done, in the wind, earthquake and fire, but God spoke to him in a gentle whisper and gave him three tasks: to anoint Hazael king over Aram, Jehu king over Israel, and Elisha to succeed him as prophet.

St Catherine's Monastery

St Catherine's Monastery was built by the Emperor Justinian during the sixth century AD on the site of an older fortified church. This first church was one of many built by Helena, the mother of the Emperor Constantine in the fourth century AD. The site is the traditional one for the burning bush (Exodus 3) and the monks show visitors a large bush said to have its roots dating back to that time! Helena had called her church after the burning bush but the name was changed to St Catherine when the body of this Egyptian martyr was found nearby. St Catherine was a virgin of noble birth martyred at Alexandria in the early fourth century AD. She died after torture tied to a wheel; hence the Catherine's wheel firework.

Helena had fortified the early church and Justinian likewise ordered that a strong wall be built round the monastery to protect it from bandits and the flood waters in the Wadi e-Deir. The walls are 40-200 ft tall. Most of the buildings date back to the sixth century AD A mosque was added in the eleventh century AD to appease the Muslim authorities and a hostel was built in the 1940s.

Prior to twentieth century AD the only entrance to St Catherine's was a small door 30 ft high, where provisions and people were lifted with a system of pulleys, and where food was often lowered to Bedouin. Such fortifications have enabled it to withstand attack and preserve its vast treasury of artifacts. (A gate has now been opened in the northwestern wall.) It is the second oldest working monastery in the world.

The monastery contains many priceless works of art from all over the world. There are Arab mosaics, marbles, western oil paintings, wax paintings, icons from Greece and Russia, and much fine metal-ware in brass, silver and gold. Until the communist revolution the church was under the patronage of the Russian Church and has among its treasures gifts from the Empress Catherine (seventeenth century AD), and the Czar Alexander (nineteenth century AD).

Its greatest asset is that its collection of illuminated manuscripts is second only to the Vatican. The collection consists of some 3,500 volumes in Hebrew, Greek, Armenian, Syriac, Georgian, Coptic, Arabic, Slavic and other languages.

Codex Sinaiticus

In 1844 a young German scholar, Tichendorf, visited St Catherine's monastery He was delighted to be able to look at their large collection of manuscripts but even more amazed when in the great hall he found a large basket full of old parchments which the monks were using as fuel for their ovens. Among these items Tichendorf found 43 pages of the Old Testament in Greek, which he was allowed to take away with him. The monks now realized that these were valuable, and when he returned for a third visit over a decade later the monks had found most of the Old Testament and the whole of the New Testament.   In Cairo, Tichendorf persuaded the Abbot of St Catherine's monastery to let him copy the book and then in 1859 the Czar of Russia was given the original. In 1933 it was sold by the Soviet government to the British Museum for £100,000, which in those days was a massive sum and had to be raised by public subscription.   The Codex Sinaiticus stands alongside the Codex Vaticanus as the two earliest complete manuscripts of the New Testament dating back to the fourth century AD.

In 1975 the monks were clearing up from a fire which had destroyed a chapel and found an old cell. In it, under the rubble of centuries, were a large number of manuscripts, many dating back over a millennium. Who knows what will be discovered next?

 The main Basilica is dedicated to St Mary. It has a nave, two aisles and an apse. Among its contents are the marble reliquary containing the bones of St Catherine and a sixth century AD mosaic of the Transfiguration in the apse. There are many wall decorations and hundreds of icons, lamps and other objects.   Note the sixth century AD inner wooden doors. The outer doors date from the eleventh century AD.

The Chapel of the Burning Bush has blue tiled walls and the Refectory has a sixteenth century AD mural of the Last Supper and carved doors from the Crusader period.

Edom

Edom, sometimes called Seir, covered an area about 100 miles long each side of the rift valley that runs from the Dead Sea to the Gulf of Aq'aba. Most of Edom is very mountainous, with the highest point being Mount Seir at 3,500 ft above the valley. The name 'Edom' derives from 'red' and may relate to the red sandstone of the area. Genesis says it was called Edom after the red stew offered by Jacob to Esau (Genesis 25:30). Most of Edom was wild with rugged mountains and steep valleys. It was semi-desert and only suitable for nomadic herding.

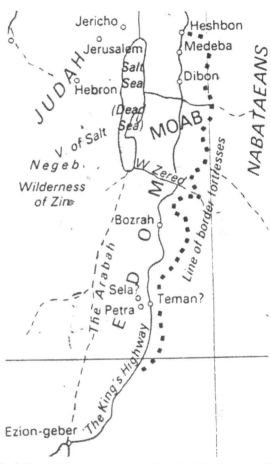

The area around the capital Bozrah (near modern-day Tafila) was well irrigated and supported the main village population.

There are a few passages in the Bible which refer to the area west of the rift valley (e.g. Numbers 34:3f) but the vast majority refer, as we will, to the area to the east.

The Israelites regarded the Edomites as close relatives, descendants of Esau, Jacob's brother (Genesis 19:30f). So Amos later refers to them as the 'brother' of Israel (Amos 1:11f). History shows that the hostility of the twin brothers, Jacob and Esau, was to continue down the centuries.

On their journey from Egypt to the Promised Land, Moses asked King Kadesh of Edom for permission to pass through their territory. The request was refused and the Edomites mustered a large army to block their way (Numbers 20f). So the Israelites skirted round Edom. This event is often quoted as the reason for continuing hostilities. However, much of the conflict also had to do with the fact that Edom was a constant threat to Judah's frontier, and moreover blocked Judean access to the Gulf of Aq'aba.

Doeg the Edomite was the chief of Saul's herdsmen (1 Samuel 22). His report about David's visit to the priests at Nob led to Saul asking Doeg to kill Ahimelech with 84 other priests. Doeg also seems to have taken it upon himself to kill everyone in the town of Nob, including infants and livestock.

David certainly avenged that act. He defeated the Edomites in the Valley of Salt and then sent his army under Joab for six months into Edom with the intention of wiping out any resistance (2 Samuel 8:12f). Hadad, a member of the royal family, escaped to Egypt where the Pharaoh was so pleased with him that he gave him his sister as a wife. Hadad returned to Edom in Solomon's reign and seems to have led periodic attacks against the Israelite forces (I Kings 11:14f).

Moab rebelled in the time of King Joram of Israel (ninth century BC) and Joram persuaded King Jehoshaphat of Judah and the king of Edom to launch an attack against the Moabites through the desert of Edom. Disaster loomed for the three kings until Elisha was called to give God's advice. The next morning water was flowing over the red soil. Knowing their long hostility with each other the Moabites thought that the three kings had fought among themselves. But when the Moabites arrived at the camp they discovered their mistake and were defeated (2 Kings 3). However, this seems to have been an isolated case of friendship and the age-long hostilities soon continued.

So by the time of the exile (sixth century BC) the prophet Obadiah castigates Edom for assisting the Babylonians and handing over to them Israelites who had fled into their territory.

Petra, although in Edom, is not mentioned in the Bible. In the eighth century King Amaziah of Judah defeated the Edomites and took Sela. Some have identified this place with Petra but that is unlikely. The most probable site is that known today as as-Sil, just north of Bozrah.

Aq'aba: Ezion Geber

The actual site of the Ezion Geber of the Bible is not known. It was probably at or near the present town of Aq'aba and may have moved its site over the centuries.

It is first mentioned in Numbers 33:35 where we read that the Israelites under Moses 'left Abronah and camped at Ezion Geber'. Moses in Deuteronomy 2:8 adds: 'So we went on past our brothers the descendants of Esau, who live in Seir. We turned from the Arabah road, which comes up from Elath and Ezion Geber, and travelled along the desert road of Moab'.

We next hear of Ezion Geber in the reign of Solomon when he visited the area and built ships there on the shore of the Red Sea. Hiram of Tyre provided experienced sailors and the ships brought back around fourteen tons of gold (1 Kings 9:26; 2 Chronicles 8:17). The port was destroyed by Shishak of Egypt when he invaded Judah in the reign of Rehoboam, Solomon's son. A hundred years later, in the ninth century BC, King Jehoshaphat of Judah made an alliance with King Ahaziah of Israel to build a fleet of trading ships to go to Ophir for gold, but they never set sail as they were wrecked at Ezion Geber (1 Kings 22:48).

There have been some finds from the Persian period (fifth century BC) and from Nabatean and Roman occupation, when the port was known as Aila or Aelana. The Romans built a road up the valley to Ma'an and Petra. The Muslims built a fort to protect Egyptians pilgrims on their way to Mecca. In the tenth century AD it was described as a great port and market. It suffered at the hands of Saladin (twelfth century AD) and remained in decay until the Turks took over in 1892. In 1917 Lawrence of Arabia and the Hejaz army led a surprise attack from the mainland. From 1925-46 it was under British control until it was handed over to the Jordanian government. Britain continued its interest, working with the Jordanians to improve the port and road and air links with the north. The Gulf of Aq'aba, part of the Red Sea and the rift valley, is a dangerous shipping lane. The entrance to the Gulf is narrow, there are many coral reefs, and there is a danger of sudden squalls, so Aq'aba has never become a large port.

The world's oldest church.
After four seasons of excavations of the Roman Aq'aba Project, archaeologists working under Dr Thomas Parker of North Carolina State University excavated what could be the oldest church in Jordan and possibly the oldest in the world. It is situated on the east side of Istiklal Road, opposite the bus station.

Archaeologists discovered a rectangular building constructed from mud bricks in the late third century AD. The area of the building is 26 metres east to west by 16 metres north to south and is oriented. The building is four metres high with a stone-built staircase, which suggests that it had a second level, which was common in the churches of that time. The doors of the building are arch-shaped. A rectangular-shaped apse, with two sacristries and oriented to the east, was discovered at the east part of the building.

Although Aq'aba was hit by several major earthquakes (AD 363 and 747) due to it being on the Jordan Rift Valley Zone, the church was buried under debris and soil which protected it from destruction and falling until it was discovered recently.

Evidence for the early date is that it is known there was a Bishop of Ayla (Aq'aba), a flourishing Roman port, by the council of Nicea in AD 325. What is likely to be a cross is painted on the white plaster walls of the nave. Fragments of glass oil lamps used by churches were found on the floor. It was close to a Christian cemetery with 24 tombs.

Kings' Highway

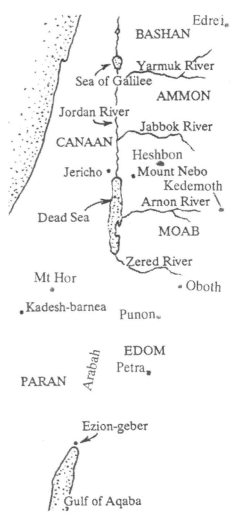

After leaving Kadesh the Israelites under Moses went 15 miles north-east to Mount Hor (Jebal Madurah) where Aaron died. Then, passing down the rift valley, they returned to Ezion Geber (Aq'aba), and asked permission from the Edomites to travel along the Kings' Highway (Numbers 20:17). This road, running from Damascus to the Gulf of Aq'aba, had been used by the Mesopotamian kings when they invaded in the time of Abraham (Genesis 14) but had been out of regular use for around 500 years. Now in the thirteenth century BC it was well guarded by the kingdoms of Edom, Moab and Ammon. They had built a series of villages, and around them a thriving settled agricultural community.

The Edomites refused permission for the Israelites to use the highway (Numbers 20:14ff) so they were compelled to make a long detour round the Edomite territory. This provoked considerable criticism of Moses by the people and led to the incident with the poisonous snakes (Numbers 21:5ff). God told Moses to make a bronze snake and put it up on a pole so that anyone who was bitten could look at it and live. Jesus referred to this incident in John 3:14-15, 'so the Son of Man must be lifted up, that everyone who believes in him may have eternal life.'

When the journey was resumed, they kept on a route close to the Edomite border and seem to have been able to buy food and water from them (Deuteronomy 2:6). They continued up the desert road, passing the Punon mines and resting for a while at the oasis of Oboth.

Crossing the Zered (Wadi-el-Hesa) between Edom and Moab they again kept to the desert side, once more avoiding Moabite hostility by keeping on the edge of the desert.

However, when they reached the north of Moabite territory at the Arnon gorge (Wadi Mojib) they seem to have decided that they would no longer avoid conflict. Up to now they had been passing by land under the control of related tribes. Now they faced Sihon the Amorite, king of Heshbon, and his country. In Deuteronomy 2:26ff we read that Moses sent messengers from the desert of Kedemoth to Sihon, seeking permission to use the Kings' Highway and to purchase food and water from the Amorites, but was refused. At the battle of Jahaz, Sihon and his army were defeated, and the Israelites went on to take their towns, from Aroer on the rim of the Arnon gorge to as far north as the Yarmuk river, near present-day Amman.

Og, King of Bashan, marched out to meet them at the battle of Edrei (Deuteronomy 3:1) and was likewise defeated. Bashan covered an area from the Yarmuk to Mount Hermon (roughly 45 miles in length). This area, along with that of the Amorites, now passed into Israelite hands. The land was good for grazing and so it was allotted to the tribes of Reuben, Gad and the half-tribe of Manasseh. Transjordan proved difficult to defend, and it was only under King David that they seem to have had a settled border.

The Israelites were now camped in the hills overlooking Jericho and the Jordan valley to the west. It was here that God gave Moses an opportunity to look out over the Promised Land from Mount Nebo before he handed over command to Joshua and died.

Near Petra the guides will point out the traditional burial site of Aaron and the spring of Moses. Both sites are unlikely to be genuine as they are too far inside Edomite territory.

Nabatea

The Nabateans began infiltrating Edom from the fifth century BC. They seem to have been a nomadic tribe living in the north-west of the Arabian peninsula and they are mentioned as enemies of Ashurbanipal of Assyria in the seventh century BC. There could also be a reference to the Egyptians trying to stop their piracy in the Red Sea area, but other than that we have no records. They probably flourished by attacking camel caravans on the Arabian trade routes before moving west to occupy the better lands of the Edomites.

Although they came from the Arabian peninsula, the Nabateans soon gave up their language and adopted the Aramaic script of the Persian empire. They also adopted the Syrian gods.

The Nabateans made Petra their capital in the fourth century BC. At the time there does not seem to have been much in the way of permanent buildings, so they may have continued to live in tents. The Greek general Antigonus, who succeeded Alexander the Great in Syria, dispatched a force of 4,000 troops under the command of Athenaeus to subdue Petra. He took the town while the defenders were at some event nearby, and carried off a considerable quantity of loot. The Nabateans soon returned and ambushed the Greek army, of which only fifty escaped. Demetrius was sent to avenge the defeat but this time the Nabateans were forewarned and seem to have emptied Petra of anything of value. Eventually Demetrius was bought off and returned to Syria with costly gifts.

Left to continue their control of the major caravan routes from India to the west, the Nabateans grew in wealth and influence. Interestingly, they also developed a sophisticated system of irrigation and crop management.

From Petra they continued pushing northward as far as Madeba. In 85 BC Damascus requested a ruler from the Nabateans. They responded but were soon attacked by Pompey's general Scaurus, who extracted 300 talents as tribute. Pompey gave Nabatea to Cleopatra and she appointed Herod to govern the area. He defeated the Nabateans when they refused to pay taxes.

Nabatean power reached its zenith under King Aretas IV (9 BC to AD 40). In his time their culture flourished alongside expanding influence over the trade routes, and they consolidated their power by building such towns as the desert city of Shivta. By the time of Paul their influence had spread to the control of Damascus. We read that Paul managed to escape the governor appointed by King Aretas by being let down over the wall in a basket (2 Corinthians 11:32ff).

King Maliku, or Malchus, assisted Vespasian when he invaded Palestine to crush the Jewish revolt in AD 66, but by then the Nabatean influence was in decline. In AD 106 Trajan's forces took Petra. Looking back we can see that, in his quest for conquest, Trajan had made a mistake. The dependency of Nabatea could have formed a vital protection against invasion from the east. Instead, the Nabatean lands that extended south into the Sinai peninsula and east as far as Luce Come became the Roman province of Arabia Petraea. Damascus and its neighbourhood were transferred to become part of the Province of Syria. Soon the Nabateans, who had risen from a desert nomadic life to one of wealth, power and sophistication, returned again to obscurity, leaving Petra as a monument to their heyday.

What happened to the Edomites?

By the fourth century BC Edom was in decline and the whole area to the east of the rift valley was infiltrated by Nabateans. Some Edomites stayed and were integrated within Nabatea. Many others fled west to southern Judea (known later under the Romans as Idumaea, with its administrative centre at Lachish).

The Maccabees, second century BC, compelled them to be circumcised and integrated into the Jewish nation. Herod the Great was the son of the Idumean ruler Antipater. Herod's mother, Kypros, was a Nabatean. Consequently he, and his family, were never fully accepted by the Jewish people. Herod fled to Petra at the time of the Parthian attack on Jerusalem in 40 BC but was not given shelter and had to flee to Rome. Herod Antipas married the daughter of King Aretas IV of Nabatea, but soured that relationship when he divorced her in favour of his niece and sister-in-law Herodias (Matthew 14:3).

Petra

Petra was the principal city of the Nabateans, and is located south of the Dead Sea in one of the most inaccessible places in that region. It is built in a deep basin high in the mountains, surrounded on every side by brilliantly coloured granite and sandstone cliffs. There is no clear refer -ence to it in the Bible although it was an important centre in New Testament times.

Petra had been built by the Nabateans, who had moved to it from the Arabian peninsula. The Nabateans retained their links with that area and made Petra a centre for trade. Through Petra from Arabia came consignments of incense for the markets of Gaza and Damascus. In exchange, the camel trains took back pottery, glass and metalwork from the west. The map below shows how Petra was built up as the hub in this trade.

The Romans took Petra in AD 106 and from then on it went into decline. Bedouin continued living there, but earthquakes and their preference for living in tents or caves meant that any building fell into decline. In 1812 a young Swiss traveller, Burckhardt, brought news of it to the west. However, even in the 1960s the site was supervised by one soldier in a small guard room near the entrance to the Siq, where there was a perfectly adequate car park for the half dozen cars that might reach such an isolated spot.. Today many hotels have followed the building of the 'Petra Resthouse' and commercialization is rapidly taking over.

The only entrance to the city is by the Siq, a narrow, mile-long gorge between towering red granite cliffs. In places the gorge is only a twelve-foot-wide stream-bed, which eventually opens out into a wider valley called Wadi Musa. This valley gradually descends into the area occupied by the 'rose-red city' half as old as time.

A visit to Petra begins at the visitors' centre. Out of the general guide books, the *Footprint* guide gives a detailed description (pages 169 – 83). *The Lonely Planet* guide has a better general map but less information on pages 176-82. The description that follows here is intended to give a brief introduction.

It is possible to take a horse from the centre down the valley of the Wadi Musa to the entrance of the Siq. However, many prefer to leave that luxury for the uphill homeward journey! Horse-drawn carriages can be hired for those who find walking difficult, and are well worth it so that you can save your energy for the site itself. Halfway down the wadi we pass the Obelisk tomb on the left.

At the top of the Siq, a dam has been built to divert the river through the Al-Muthlim tunnel and into the Wadi Muthlim near the Eagle monument. Although the riverbed is usually dry, a flash flood killed 23 tourists in 1963, so it was decided the tunnel was needed for the safety of future visitors.

The Siq was the main defence for Petra. Walking down this narrow gorge – sometimes it is only ten feet wide – it is easy to imagine how a few soldiers on the cliffs above could prevent any advance below. There are some very interesting rock formations but it is best to look at these on the return journey when the sun is in the west and one is more in need of rest stops!

Al Khazneh Pharon (Pharaoh's treasury) is one of the world's most famous pictures. Try and imagine what it was like for those entering without such a preview! Dr Hoskins made such a journey recorded in the National Geographic magazine (May 1907). He writes,

> We picked our way into this matchless defile (the Siq). We wandered on amazed, enchanted and delighted, not wishing for, not expecting, that anything could be finer than this, when a look ahead warned us that we were approaching some monument worth attention, and suddenly we stepped our of the narrow gorge into the sunlight again. There in front of us, carved in the face of the cliff, half revealed, half concealed in the growing shadows, one of the largest, most perfect, and most beautiful monuments of antiquity – Pharaoh's Treasury – a royal temple-tomb carved out of the rock wall.

The tomb is best visited at around 10am. It is 150 feet high and adorned by many finely carved Corinthian columns. On its apex is a massive, artistically designed urn. Within the temple is a tomb-room of moderate size that is without ornamentation. No one knows to whom the temple-tomb belonged, but it is regarded as the tomb of a Nabatean king , perhaps King Aretas the Philhellene (87-62 BC).

The plan opposite shows

1 The treasury
2 Various small tombs
3 Tomb of Uneishu
4 Streets of facades
5 Theatre

The Tomb of Uneisha is opposite the theatre. Uneisha was an important member of the household of the most powerful of the Nabatean kings, Aretas IV, referred to by Paul in 2 Corinthians 11:32. It is a very good example of a royal tomb.

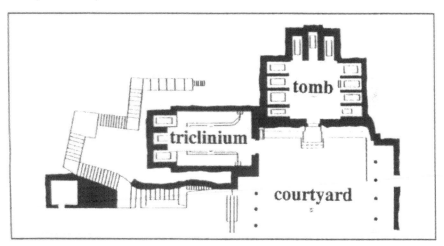

Leaving the royal tombs up the hill to our right, we turn left down the road containing the main Roman ruins. Like the theatre we will see more extensive examples elsewhere. (*Footprint* guide has a good plan of this area.)

As we come to the end of the Roman road we turn to the right and reach the *Forum Restaurant.* This is one of several such facilities now available in Petra.

After a rest and refreshments it is time to decide between three options for the afternoon, probably with the help of a donkey!
- A leisurely return with a closer look at the royal tombs.
- A climb up to Ed-Deir (The Monastery).
- A climb up to the Jabal Madbah.

The way up to Ed Deir is fairly clear but I have given details of the others as sometimes these are visited without a guide.

The royal tombs
These tombs are on the hillside facing one from the Roman road.

6 Khubtha high places.
7 Urn tomb – in the fifth century AD it was used as a church by the Bishop of Petra. It is now known locally as the prison.
8 Silk tomb - notice the swirling patterns in the rock.
9 Corinthian tomb – a mix of styles with the top similar to the treasury.
10 Palace tomb – possibly modelled on a Roman palace.

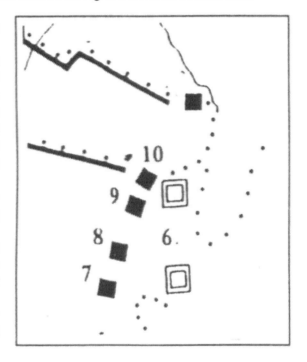

Jabal Madbah (High Place)   The climb to the High Place passes more tombs than that to the Ed Deir but involves a steeper climb.

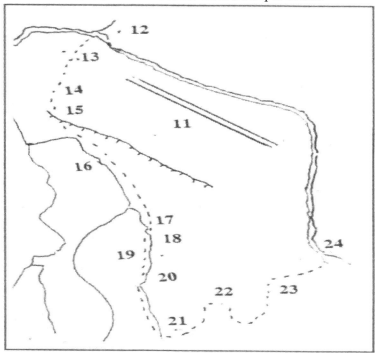

11 Roman road.
12 Forum Restaurant.
13 Small museum in tomb.
14 Columbarium where cremation urns were stored.
15 City wall.
16 Wadi Farasa (horse) − be sure to follow this wadi close to the hill on your left.
17 Broken Pediment tomb − simple Nabatean design with swirling
.... patterns in the sandstone.
18 Renaissance tomb − a very fine example with pilasters and arch.
19 Roman soldier tomb − the central figure clearly wears Roman armour.
20 Garden tomb − the garden in front is the triclinium (a banqueting hall in
...... honour of the dead).
21 Lion fountain − it is likely that the water was channelled in a fountain out of the lion's mouth.
22 High Place − see the guide book descriptions.
23 Steps down to 24 − tomb of Uneisha on our earlier route.

Moab

Moab was a small kingdom along the Kings' Highway between Edom and Ammon, located between the Brook Zered (Wadi el-Hesa) and the Arnon (Wadi el-Mujib). The kingdom existed from around 1300 to 600 BC. The main town today is Kerak.

In other ancient texts Moab is known as *ma'aba* or *mu'aba*. The Israelites may have used Moab as a derogatory name linking with Genesis 19:37 where Lot's oldest daughter named her son Moab.

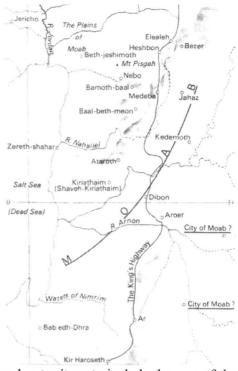

Bible History

Throughout her history, Moab was in conflict with her neighbours, sometimes extending her territory to include the area of the former kingdom of Ammon, sometimes under the control of other nations like the Israelites under David. Its role as an independent state seems to have ended in the time of the Babylonian invasion in the early sixth century BC.

The Moabites feared that the Israelites, to whom they had refused permission to use the Kings' Highway, would seek to overrun their new kingdom. So King Balak of Moab hired Balaam, a diviner from Mesopotamia, to pronounce a curse upon Israel. The story is vividly told in Numbers 22-24 and is noted for Balaam's ass!

For a brief period (Judges 3) King Eglon of Moab invaded Israelite land on both sides of the River Jordan. After Eglon's assassination by Ehud, the Moabites seem to have retreated south of the Arnon and peace was restored.

The soil of Moab has always had the potential to produce good crops. Throughout its existence Moab relied on a mixed economy of arable crops – wheat and barley – and sheep-rearing, an economy similar to that of today. Like the rest of the region it is susceptible to drought, but it sometimes retained its fertility while Israel suffered famine. During one such time Naomi and her family moved to Moab (Ruth 1). There she lost her husband and sons but returned home with Ruth, who later became the grandmother of King David (Ruth 4:17).

Solomon had Moabite women in his harem and built a centre for the worship of their god Chemosh (1 Kings 11). Isaiah (15:16), Jeremiah (9:25, 48:1f), Amos (2:1f) and Zephaniah (2:8ff) all proclaim God's judgment on Moab and refer to towns which at that time were under her control: Nebo, Medeba, Heshbon, Dibon, Ar, Kir and Horonaim. At this time Kerak - Kir-haroseth was noted for its vineyards.

A weak and small state meant that Moab was often in conflict with her neighbours, and she finally fell to the Babylonians in the early sixth century BC. Later the area was under the control of the Nabateans and Romans before falling to the forces of Islam.

Moabite Stone   This black basalt stela was found at Dhiban in the 1860s.   It contained thirty-four lines of inscriptions about the military victories over Israel and the building work of King Mesha of Moab in the ninth century BC.   The inscription reads: 'I am Mesha, son of ... king of Moab, the Dibonite. My father ruled over Moab thirty years, and I became king after my father. I made this high place for Chemosh ... because he delivered me from all ... and caused me to triumph over my enemies. Omri, King of Israel, had oppressed Moab many days because Chemosh was angry with his land ...'.

Ammon

The Ammonites claimed the territory east of the Dead Sea and the River Jordan from the River Arnon to the River Jabbok (Nahr as-Zarqa). However, it is hard to find evidence that, except for a few years, they controlled much more than an area around Amman and lands to its east.

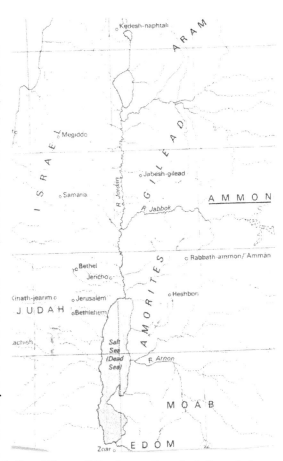

The Ammonites, like the Moabites, were related to the Israelites through Lot. They were commanded not to attack them except in self-defence (Deuteronomy 2:19). In the time of Moses most of the Ammonite territory was in the hands of Sihon, king of the Amorites and Og, King of Bashan. Israel defeated these kings and occupied their land.

Jabbok   The River Jabbok (Nahr as-Zarqa) is crossed just north of Al-Mustaba, about ten miles south of Jerash. Here Jacob, on his way to meet his estranged brother Esau, sends his family ahead of him across the stream and then spends the night wrestling with God. In the morning he names the place Peniel (Genesis 33:22ff).

During the time of the Judges, the Ammonites sought to extend their territory. Saul drove them back from Jabesh-Gilead and on that reputation was appointed king (1 Samuel 11ff).

Their King Nahash was a friend of David. When Nahash died, David sent a delegation to offer sympathy to his son Hanun, but the new king insulted the men by cutting off half of their beards. So David sent Joab to punish them and a battle took place at Medeba. The Ammonites' allies, the Arameans, deserted them, leaving the Ammonites to flee (2 Samuel 10). While Joab was laying siege to their capital, Rabbah (Amman), David arranged for Uriah to be killed, so enabling him to marry Uriah's wife Bathsheba (2 Samuel 11).

Solomon included Ammonite women in his harem and they brought with them the worship of their gods Molech and Chemosh (1 Kings 11). Like many of the surrounding religions, worship of these gods included human sacrifice.

In 2 Chronicles 20 Jehoshaphat was enabled by God to win a great victory. Instead of commanding the Israelites to attack, he ordered them to 'praise the Lord'. To the Israelites amazement, the Ammonites, Moabites and men from Mount Seir (Edom) started fighting among themselves until no one was left. It took the Israelites three days to collect all the plunder.

After the exile in Babylon, Tobiah the Ammonite joined others in opposing the rebuilding of the walls of Jerusalem (Nehemiah 2). His family, the Tobiads, were still influential in the region until the time of Alexander the Great.

Christians in Transjordan

In the third century AD the Emperor Diocletian reorganized the empire. He realized that the eastern frontiers were vulnerable and so built a new line of camps along the border with Arabia (Lineas Arabicus). Many soldiers were enlisted in their teens. They were allowed to marry local girls, and before long these camps were surrounded by villages of their wives, children, retired soldiers and other workers. When Christianity became a legal religion, many adopted the faith and churches were built in the villages. Madaba is a good example.

The town prospered in Nabatean and Roman times. Its bishop was present at Chalcedon in AD 451. By the sixth century there were at least fourteen churches in Madaba, most of which had fine mosaic floors.

When the Arabs invaded in the seventh century the soldiers moved into the private houses and took up farming and related trades. Gradually they shifted into a nomadic lifestyle. The oldest Bedouin clans in Jordan come from these early Christians, and even today one can stop at a Bedouin tent in the middle of the desert and discover that they are Christians. Some moved into places like Petra where Christian symbols can still be found in buildings that were used for worship.

Medeba – Madaba in the Bible

The town is about 20 miles south of Amman on the Kings' Highway and Roman Road between Dibon and Heshbon.

At Madaba, Israel, under Moses, defeated Sihon, King of the Amorites. Madaba was assigned to the tribe of Reuben (Joshua 13:9f). Here David defeated an Aranaean army hired by the Amorites (1 Chronicles 19:7). The Moabite King Mesha rebuilt Madaba in the eighth century BC and the place is mentioned in Isaiah's prophesy against Moab (Isaiah 15:2).

In the second century BC Madaba was in the hands of Jambri and his family who seized and killed John Maccabeus. John Hycanus took the town after a six-month siege.

In the mid-nineteenth century the Christian Bedouin started to settle in towns. As they did not attempt any mission to the local Muslims, there does not seem to have been more than isolated opposition to this.

The first major problem arose in 1896 when the Franciscans set up a mission in Kerak (Kerak still has a small Melkite church and a larger Franciscan presence). The Catholic mission began to seek the conversion of the Muslim population, and that led to riots. The Melkite/Orthodox Christians in Kerak decided to leave, and obtained permission to join a group of Christian Bedouin who were living in the ruins of Madaba.

As more Christians moved into Madaba they began to build more churches. One such church was built on an early fifth century AD Byzantine church with a large mosaic floor. The builders decided to put in a modern slab floor and started to break up the mosaics, but fortunately the librarian of the Greek Orthodox church in Jerusalem was visiting at the time and managed to save about a third of the precious floor.

The mosaics in the Church of St George, at Madaba, give us an interesting insight into the attitude of Orthodox Christians living in the Muslim lands. Basically it is to keep in a Christian ghetto, affirming their faith but not attempting to evangelise Muslims. Until recently Muslims have tended to reciprocate, although there is now a move towards seeking the conversion of Christians to Islam. So we see the Orthodox commitment to God in the Madaba map, which was made after the Muslim invasion. The map shows the land still under the control of the Christian sees (or dioceses). There is no sign on the map of the Dome of the Rock or the Aksa mosque. The Muslims had sought to show their superiority by hiring Christian craftsmen to build these slightly larger than the Church of the Holy Sepulchre, which in those days was twice its present size. So the Dome of the Rock is about half a metre higher than the dome in the Church of the Holy Sepulchre. Instead of competing, the map ignores such claims.

To conclude Madaba's history, we note that, at the time of the formation of the State of Israel, many Palestinian refugees moved into Madaba and today the majority of its people are Muslims.

Christians are a small minority in Jordan. The main churches are the Greek Orthodox, as in Madaba, and the Roman Catholics in Kerak. Amman has several other denominations brought in by missionaries from the West.

Madaba map

The map is divided up into the various sees (or dioceses) of the Christian Church. It is a clear statement that Christ rules.
Places with a bishopric are highlighted. Holy sites and churches are marked by using red stone. There are many inscriptions about the sites taken from the old or New Testaments.

The original map measured 78 x 20 ft. It contained over 2.5 million stones. Only one third of it has survived.

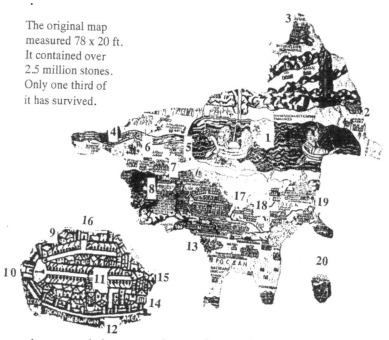

Across the centre it is easy to locate the Dead Sea [1]. Boats there are carrying salt and asphalt. The sailors have been defaced in deference to the Muslim ban on depicting the human form.

To the east, just above the Dead Sea, is Lot [2]. Herod died there at the hot springs. It was the centre of a bishopric, a monastery and regarded as a holy place. (The site can be visited today, signposted Al Mukhayyat on the Madaba to Nebo road.)

The large place to the east and at the top edge of the remaining map is Kerak [3].

Returning to the river Jordan [4] flowing into the Dead Sea, we note that a fish, having tasted the Dead Sea water, is retreating up stream!

To the west , one of the baptism sites (Bethabara) is shown [5] as is Gilgal [6] with its twelve stones (Joshua 4:20).

Nearby is Jericho IEPIXW [7] and then moving due west into the highlands (darker stone) note the red roof on Jacob's well (John 4) [8].

Moving south we come to Jerusalem [9]. The cardo (or main street) runs from north to south, starting at the Damascus gate with its pillar [10].
Halfway along the cardo is the church of the Holy Sepulchre [11]. In those days it was twice the size, with a large atrium and church reaching down to the cardo. The present church (half the size) dates from the eleventh and twelfth century restorations. Further west is the small Jaffa gate[12]. Jaffa town is due west at the coast [13]. Moving south we find the Church of Mount Zion and Justinian's great church to Mary, the mother of our Lord, built in AD 540 [14]. The Dung gate leads out with steps to the City of David [15] and then moving north again on the other side of the cardo we see the Church of the Pinnacle on the Holy Mount, the Golden Gate (note no sign of the temple mount) and the larger gate of St Stephen [16] now called the Lion Gate.

Moving south of Jerusalem we see the Akeldama (field of blood) [17] (Acts 1:19). Then we have Bethlehem written in red with a small church [18] and Hebron [19].

Moving due west the map has been lost, so Ashkelon [20] looks like an island.

The last two letters 'ZA' of Gaza [21], a large city with many red roofs can be seen, near the place that Philip baptized the Ethiopian eunuch.

To the south-east of Gaza are the hills of Sinai [22] and then the Nile Delta with its many churches [23].

Nebo

In Deuteronomy 32:49 God commands Moses, 'Go up into the Abarim Range to Mount Nebo in Moab, across from Jericho, and view Canaan, the land I am giving the Israelites as their own possession.' Later we read chapter 34:

> Moses climbed Mount Nebo from the plains of Moab to the top of Pisgah, across from Jericho. There the Lord showed him the whole land ... from the Valley of Jericho, the City of Palms, as far as Zoar. Then the Lord said to him, 'This is the land I promised on oath to Abraham, Isaac and Jacob when I said, "I will give it to your descendants." I have let you see it with your eyes, but you will not cross over into it.' And Moses the servant of the Lord died there in Moab, as the Lord had said. He buried him in Moab, in the valley opposite Beth Peor, but to this day no one knows where his grave is. Moses was a hundred and twenty years old when he died, yet his eyes were not weak nor his strength gone. The Israelites grieved for Moses in the plains of Moab thirty days, until the time of weeping and mourning was over (Deuteronomy 34).

Nebo

The Hebrew name is linked to the word meaning 'proclaimer'. The mountain should not be confused with

• The village of Nebo nearby, probably now known as Mekhayyat (Numbers 32:3). It was held by the tribes of Reuben and Gad until, as the Moabite stone records, it was recaptured by King Mesha of Moab in 850 BC.

• The Children of Nebo (Ezra 2:29) are probably from the village of Nob (Beit Nubah) about 7 miles north of Hebron.

• Nebo is also used for an Assyrian god (Isaiah 46:1) whose temple lies in ruins at Birs Nimrud.

Mount Nebo is therefore an important site to Jews, Christians and Muslims, all of whom regard Moses as a prophet. The probable site is Ras es-Siyagha, which is a prominent spur of the Abarim mountain range. It is twelve miles east of the mouth of the Jordan River and three miles west of Medeba. It is over 2,700 feet above sea level and 4,000ft above the Dead Sea. From this unobstructed vantage point, one can enjoy a magnificent and almost unparalleled view of much of Palestine immediately west of the Jordan.

From this same point, Moses could look down on the tents of the Israelites spread out in the valley. Earlier Balaam, at the request of King Balak of Moab, had looked down on the Israelites from a nearby vantage point (Numbers 23).

On a clear day one can stand on the terrace west of the church and see the towers on the Mount of Olives at Jerusalem, and to the north the snowcapped peaks of Hermon.

Although the Israelites never located the tomb of Moses, in the fourth century AD Christians claimed to have found the site and built a church over the empty tomb. It was called the 'small church', as next to it was one of the largest churches in the Holy Land, dedicated to St Mary. By the sixth century, Peter the Iberian found it to be 'a very large temple, named after the prophet [Moses] and many Monasteries which are built round it.' This enlarged church continued to be mentioned until 1564, when a Portuguese Franciscan monk visited the site and found the buildings on the summit ruined and abandoned.

The excavations carried on here by the Franciscans since 1933 confirm the accounts of early travellers, who came upon a small three-apsed (*cella trichora*) church. The church was enlarged during the late fifth century. Apparently it was destroyed by an earthquake in the late sixth century and rebuilt in AD 597. There are mosaics in the floor of the church, and some splendid pictures of animals and trees in one of the chapels. In the Chapel of the Virgin a floor depicts the Temple of Jerusalem with its two courtyards and altar for burnt sacrifices.

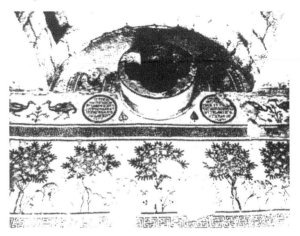

The extensive ruins of the monastery buildings cluster around the church on the west, north, and south.

Bethany beyond the Jordan

Since the signing of a peace accord between Jordan and Israel, extensive work is being carried out at this site. Christian denominations have been offered land on which to build their own church and the Archbishop of Canterbury accepted one such offer in 2008.

The site is linked with the Baptism of Jesus by John, although a few scholars still prefer a site in the north nearer to Galilee. The site is also called Beth-abara (house of crossing) and so linked with the crossing of the Jordan by the Israelites under Joshua and that of Elijah just before he was carried up to heaven in a whirlwind. If the hill on this site known as Elijah's hill was accepted as such in the first century, then it is appropriate for John, who was often associated with Elijah, to choose this place for his work.

It is also thought that this site is close to the fords of the Jordan at Beth-Barah (Judges 7:24-25) where Gideon defeated the Midianites and where Jephthah tested whether a person could correctly pronounce *shibboleth*. The Ephraimites said *sibboleth* and Jephthah's men killed all who made that mispronunciation. The Madaba map locates this as a crossing-site.

Also on this rapidly growing site is a small area of natural forest. The pride of Jordan (Zechariah 11:3) was well known in Bible times for its dense woodland of willow, poplar and tamarisk trees. Until recently wild animals were found living there including lions, tigers, bears, hyenas, jackals and otters. Jeremiah used these common sightings in his prophecies against Edom and Babylon (49:19; 50:44)

So this small area was named and renamed many times as various events took place or were remembered during the time of the early church. There are now many locations on this site so most visits are limited to certain key places.

There seems good reason to accept this as the most likely site for John to be baptizing. As it was close to the fords of the Jordan, many visitors to Jerusalem from Galilee or from the Kings' Highway would be crossing nearby and would carry the news of his ministry to Jerusalem. We read in Matthew that 'People went out to him from Jerusalem and all Judea and the whole region of the Jordan. Confessing their sins, they were baptized by him in the Jordan River' (Matthew 3:5).

There may be some evidence that baptisms took place at Wadi Kharrar a small tributary of the Jordan river that is fed by five springs. The water would have been cleaner and also less dangerous, as the Jordan of those days was a fast flowing river in the rainy season.

A large church east of the river dates from the late Byzantine period. It has fine coloured stone pavements and mosaics and columns with Corinthian capitals. It may have been built where it was believed Jesus was baptized. It is also likely to be the church of an early saint, St Mary the Egyptian. She was a prostitute who was converted through a voice from God in the Church of the Holy Sepulchre and then lived by the Jordan for 47 years before she died.

Hermits and monks continued to live in the nearby caves and a monastery was built (fifth century). An inscription reads 'By the help and grace of Christ our God the whole monastery was constructed in the time of Rhotorius, the most God beloved Abbot. May God the Saviour grant him mercy.'

Sketch plan of Bethany-beyond-the-Jordan

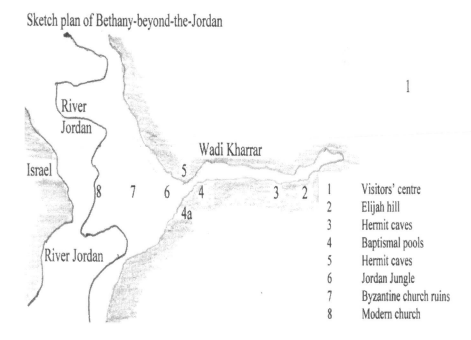

1	Visitors' centre
2	Elijah hill
3	Hermit caves
4	Baptismal pools
5	Hermit caves
6	Jordan Jungle
7	Byzantine church ruins
8	Modern church

The Dead Sea

Although Europeans have named it the Dead Sea, the Bible normally refers to it as the Salt Sea (Genesis 14:3; Numbers 34:3; Joshua 3:16), so linking it with its most important commodity, salt. The New Testament does not mention it because it does not feature in any of the incidents recorded during that time.

The sea is 53 miles long, up to 10 miles wide, and as much as 1,200 feet deep, whilst its shoreline is the lowest area on earth not covered by water (1,300ft below sea level).

The barrenness of the region goes back far into history. However, terraces of alluvial deposits in the deep valley of the Jordan show that formerly one great lake extended from north Galilee to well south of the present 'sea'. The waters were then about 1,400 feet above the present level of the Dead Sea, or slightly above that of the Mediterranean, and at that time were much less salt.   This was well before the time of Abraham.

Up to five million tons of water enter the Dead Sea each day from the Jordan River, streams and rainy-season wadis.   However, the sea possesses no outlet for this water except evaporation, which is very high in the summer when the temperatures at water-level are often over 40° C. Most of the streams which feed the Dead Sea are highly saline, flowing through nitrous soils, and springs beside and under it contain high levels of sulphur, bromine, magnesium and calcium.   In the south-east corner there is a 1,500 metre-deep salt plug. These and other factors combine to produce a salinity of around 26 per cent, the average seawater salinity being 3.5 per cent. This makes the Dead Sea the earth's most saline body of water, with an ever-increasing solidity.

Mineral extraction has taken place throughout its history. In Bible times the two main industries were salt and bitumen. Today the main factories are for the processing of potash for fertilizers.

Sodom and Gomorrah are likely to have been at the southern end of the sea, and archaeologists have confirmed that there were many towns in this area at the time of Abraham.   The natural elements which God used in his judgment (Genesis 19) are likely to have been an explosion of the subsurface bituminous layers.   Karstic salt pillars, known as Lot's wife, are commonplace.   Here, as in other instances, the intervention of God was in the form of sending a warning of disaster, with the refusal to heed it leading to loss of life. Many natural disasters today are preceded by warnings.

As the Sea formed one of Israel's borders, there is frequent mention of it in the books of Numbers, Deuteronomy and Joshua. Some examples of these are:

> Your southern side will include some of the Desert of Zin along the border of Edom. On the east, your southern boundary will start from the end of the Salt Sea (Numbers 34:3).
> It included all the Arabah east of the Jordan, as far as the Sea of the Arabah, below the slopes of Pisgah (Deuteronomy 4:49).

Perhaps the most interesting reference to the 'Sea' occurs in Ezekiel. At the end of his prophecy (chapter 47) Ezekiel has a vision of God's blessing in the form of water coming out of the temple in Jerusalem. After two miles it had become a river too deep to cross.

> This water flows toward the eastern region and goes down into the Arabah, where it enters the Sea. When it empties into the Sea, the water there becomes fresh. Swarms of living creatures will live wherever the river flows. There will be large numbers of fish, because this water flows there and makes the salt water fresh; so where the river flows everything will live. Fishermen will stand along the shore; from En Gedi to En Eglaim there will be places for spreading nets. The fish will be of many kinds - like the fish of the Great Sea. But the swamps and marshes will not become fresh; they will be left for salt. Fruit trees of all kinds will grow on both banks of the river. Their leaves will not wither, nor will their fruit fail. Every month they will bear, because the water from the sanctuary flows to them. Their fruit will serve for food and their leaves for healing (Ezekiel 47:8-12).

It is a picture of what God can do to renew us, his people, and, as a similar example of such a blessing, Israel's borders will be extended far beyond any they had enjoyed in the past (Ezekiel 47:13-23).

Decapolis

Decapolis means 'ten cities'. It is sometimes assumed that the Decapolis was a league of ten cities. However, there does not seem to have been any clear organization linking them together and their number varied from ten to eighteen. We do know that, as early as the third century BC, settlers established them to promote Greek culture, and the Romans used them as a buffer zone between the Jews and the hostile peoples of the east. Certainly they had no love for the Jews, who had attacked some of them during the time of the Maccabees. It is probably best to regard them as a group of trade centres along the three roads that connected Damascus with the south.

The second century AD writer Pliny named the ten cities as:

Damascus, which was a key trading centre with the east. It is now capital of Syria, but in Roman times the Province of Syria was administered from Antioch.

Hippos is just above En-Gev on the eastern shore of Lake Tiberius. The promontory (2 km by 500m) between two valleys was a useful stop between Bet Shean and Damascus. It was taken from the Jews by Pompey in 63 BC and rebuilt in a gridiron pattern.

Scythopolis (Bet Shean, where Saul's body was hung after his defeat by the Philistines) is the only one on the west of the Jordan and well inside Jewish territory. It was taken by Pompey for the

Decapolis and became an important centre for linen until sixth century AD.

Pella was named after the birthplace of Alexander, and was the city to which the Jewish Christians fled during the Jewish uprising that led to the destruction of Jerusalem in AD 70. It is on the other side of the Jordan valley, overlooking Scythopolis.

Philadelphia (modern Amman) was the most southerly of the cities.

Gerasa (modern Jerash) is 30 miles north of Philadelphia and by far the best preserved of the Decapolis.

Gadara is on a steep hillside dropping down into the Yarmuk valley just south of Lake Tiberius.

Dion is further up the Yarmuk valley.

Canatha is now Qanawat in Syria. The temple complex is one of the most intact buildings dating from the second century AD, which was later converted into a Christian church.

Raphana was probably between these last two and Damascus.

Ptolemy, another second-century writer, names eighteen cities in the Decapolis, omitting Raphana but adding nine others. A later source mentioned fourteen cities in the group. Thus the number varied from time to time.

Decapolis in the Bible

Jesus and his disciples crossed Lake Tiberius into the Decapolis. There he healed a man called 'legion'. As the healing resulted in a large herd of pigs rushing down and drowning in the lake, their owners, either from Geresa or Gadara, asked him to leave the district. The man who had been healed went around the Decapolis proclaiming 'how much Jesus had done for him. And all the people were amazed' (Mark 5).

In Matthew 4:25, people from the Decapolis were among a large crowd following Jesus.

After his visit to the area around Tyre and Sidon, Jesus visited the region of the Decapolis and healed the man who was deaf, using the word 'Ephphatha' (Mark 7:31ff).

Jerash

As Geraza, Jerash was one of the Decapolis towns. Although inhabited from as far back as the stone age – the town has always had a plentiful supply of fresh water – it grew into a large town in the time of the Selucids, second century BC. It was conquered by the Jews and in 63 BC by Pompey. From then on it remained under Roman rule until the fall of the empire. It was administered first under the province of Syria and then from the second century it became one of the three chief cities of the province of Arabia.

Jerash also became an important Christian centre, with twelve churches and the cathedral having so far been located. In the seventh century AD it was captured by the Persians and then by the Muslims. Although fortified briefly by the Crusaders, the city was soon deserted and covered by sand.

In 1925 Professor Garstang, with British and American funding, began the long process of clearance and restoration. His work has revealed one of the best preserved cities of the Roman world.

Jerash is a fine example of planning, with a main street about half a mile long intersected at right angles (gridiron).

Footprint gives a clear guide and plan to the site (pages 98-108).

Pella

Pella is today known as Tabaqat Fahl. It is one of the most ancient sites in Jordan. A spring Ain el-Jirm gives it an all-year-round water supply. The site has been occupied since Neolithic times (c.7000 BC) and some finds go back to the Paleolithic era.

The city is called Pihilum in Egyptian texts from around 1800 BC. Around the time of Moses it had 5,000 inhabitants and they produced the wooden spokes for the Egyptian chariots. It had trade with Egypt and Cyprus as well as its locality. Its name was changed to Pella under Greek rule, possibly because a town of the name of Pella was the birthplace of Alexander the Great. It changed hands several times during this period and was sacked by Alexander Jannaeus (c.80 BC).

It prospered after the conquest by Pompey in 63 BC and was one of the cities in the Decapolis. During the Jewish revolt of AD 66 Christians from Jerusalem under the leadership of St Simon came to Pella as a safe refuge (Matthew 24:16). In the second century Ariston, the author of the *Dialogue of Jason and Papiscos,* was born there, and there are many Christian tombs and inscriptions from that period. The strong Christian presence continued into Byzantine times and there were major building projects including two large churches. The names of only three bishops have survived: Zebennus in 449 (Council of Ephesus); Paul in 518; and Zachary in 532. At this time the population rose to around 25,000. The city continued under Muslim rule but never recovered from the devastating earthquake of AD 747.

Cathedral This basilica in the civic centre near the spring may have been part of a monastery. It was built around AD 400 and used stone from a variety of Roman buildings. Mosaics decorate the floor. The stairway used the seats from the Roman theatre and Odeum. Some columns have been re-erected. There are two other major churches: the West and the East basilicas.

If time allows it is worth seeing the Roman gate, and nearby the major trenches that have been dug by the Australian archaeologists on the main Tell (Khirbet Fahl).

Archaeologists from Australia are working on the site and their reports can be found on www.astarte.com.au. One of the latest relates to a Canaanite temple.

Gadara

Gadara was one of the most important cities of the Decapolis. It seems to have held a considerable area around it, stretching down to Lake Galilee near the hot springs of Hammath about six miles away.

So the question is, did the healing of the demon-possessed men (Matthew 8:28), take place in this area, or further north along the lakeside at Geresa (modern Kursi) or in the territory of Gerasa (Jerash). Probably we will never know and each place has its own claim to the event.

Gadara was captured by Antiochus III in 218 BC. The Maccabean Alexander Janneus captured it and it was held as part of the Jewish state until Pompey (68 BC) annexed it into the Province of Syria. Augustus gave Gadara to Herod the Great (30 BC) but he was noted for his ruthless oppression of the people, so on his death it was returned to the Province of Syria. The Jews tried to hold it again during the revolt of AD 66 but it was reoccupied by Vespasian on 21 March 68. After that it might have become a Roman colony. We know that in the second century it had a large Christian community The Bishop of Gadara attended the Council of Nicea in AD 325.

Among its well-known citizens were the poet Meleager, and the philosophers Menippus and Philidenus. Strabo notes that the pleasure-loving Romans returned to Gadara after enjoying the hot springs at Hammath down the valley. There they enjoyed the cooler heights of the city and watched plays in the theatres.

Umm Qais (Qeis) or Muqeis has been identified as the site of Gadara. It is on a headland between the Yarmuk river in the north and the Wadi Arab in the south. The main excavations were carried out by German teams in the 1970s.

If this is the site of the healing of the two men who lived in tombs, then there are two such tombs near the entrance to the site that in the past were used by Bedouin as goat houses. Also near the tombs of Germani and Modestus is one of Gadara's two theatres. This north theatre was once the larger of the two but most of its stone has been removed for other buildings. To its right are the remains of a temple, possibly to Zeus.

We now follow the old main road running from east to west, the Decumanus Maximus.

The next building of note is a church dating from the fifth century which was built on the old Roman forum. The church has basalt columns and there are two *exedrae*, one of which contains a font. Its tiled floor has fine geometric patterns. The shopping area is still visible in the barrel vaults below the forum.

The west theatre is made of black basalt. It held about 3,000 people and probably dates from the first century AD. Here is a good place to view the Lake of Galilee and the Golan Heights.

There are many other buildings on the site, including a well preserved mausoleum but this is usually kept locked.

Amman

Professor Harding, who has been largely responsible for its excavation, writes, 'in 1932 Amman was little more than an overgrown village'. So how has this change taken place?

Amman has been inhabited since Neolithic times. It was called Rabbath (or Rabbah: great) Ammon in biblical times and references to it are under *Ammon* in the Bible quotations (page 90). By the time of Moses it was a reasonably sized city importing goods from many countries. The first Bible reference is in Deuteronomy 3, where it is pointed out that the great iron bed (four metres long) of Og, King of Bashan, had been carried there as a trophy from the war between Bashan and the Ammonites.

The Israelites under Moses are unlikely to have taken Rabbath. The Ammonites continued to attack Israel during the time of the Judges and Saul. After David's forces had defeated the Ammonites they laid siege to Rabbath and it was during that seige that David had Uriah the Hittite killed so that he could marry Bathsheba (2 Samuel 10-12). The prophets Jeremiah, Ezekiel and Amos also refer to the place.

It was conquered by the Assyrians, Persians and Greeks. The Greeks renamed it Philadelphia and under Roman rule it joined the Decapolis cities.

The Bishop of Petra and Philadelphia had his base there in the Byzantine era. After the Moslem conquest and major earthquakes it was a small town. Modern Amman was reborn after Circassians (people expelled by Russia from the Caucasus) settled there in 1878 or 1887. The first four Mayors of Amman (1905–1920) were Circassians, before the establishment of Transjordan by the Hashemite Emir Abdullah.

In 1921, Abdullah I chose Amman as seat of government for his newly created state, the Emirate of Transjordan, and later as the capital of the Hashemite Kingdom of Jordan. As there was no palatial building, he started his reign from the station, with his office in a train carriage. Amman remained a small city until 1948, when the population expanded considerably due to an influx of Palestinian refugees from what is now

Israel. Amman has experienced exceptionally rapid development since 1952 under the leadership of Kings Hussein and Abdullah II.

The Roman theatre that was built to hold 6,000 people and the Citadel hill are the major remains still visible from the past. The National Archaeological Museum is at the Jabal al-Qal (Citadel hill) and nearby is the Roman temple of Hercules, built around AD 170, and the Byzantine church from around the fifth century. The main feature on the top of the citadel is the Umayyad Palace or audience hall, probably dating from the seventh century.

Amman citadel

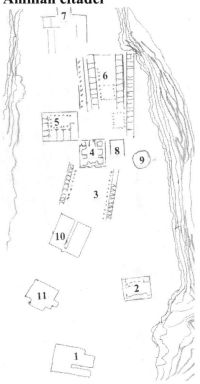

1 Temple of Hercules
2 Byzantine church
3 Umayyad market square
4 Umayyad palace with dome
5 Audience room
6 Colonnaded street
7 Throne rooms
8 Baths
9 Water cistern
10 Mosque
11 Visitors' centre and Museum

B – Bible Quotations

Egypt in the Bible

Abraham visits c.1850BC Genesis 12:10
Now there was a famine in the land, and Abram went down to Egypt to live there for a while because the famine was severe.

Joseph in Egypt c.1600 Genesis 37:28
So when the Midianite merchants came by, his brothers pulled Joseph up out of the cistern and sold him for twenty shekels of silver to the Ishmaelites, who took him to Egypt.

Genesis 39:1
Now Joseph had been taken down to Egypt. Potiphar, an Egyptian who was one of Pharaoh's officials, the captain of the guard, bought him from the Ishmaelites who had taken him there.

Genesis 41:1
When two full years had passed, Pharaoh had a dream: He was standing by the Nile,…

Genesis 41:53 – 42:3
The seven years of abundance in Egypt came to an end, and the seven years of famine began, just as Joseph had said. There was famine in all the other lands, but in the whole land of Egypt there was food. When all Egypt began to feel the famine, the people cried to Pharaoh for food. Then Pharaoh told all the Egyptians, 'Go to Joseph and do what he tells you.' When the famine had spread over the whole country, Joseph opened the storehouses and sold grain to the Egyptians, for the famine was severe throughout Egypt. And all the countries came to Egypt to buy grain from Joseph, because the famine was severe in all the world. When Jacob learned that there was grain in Egypt, he said to his sons, 'Why do you just keep looking at each other?' He continued, 'I have heard that there is grain in Egypt. Go down there and buy some for us, so that we may live and not die.' Then ten of Joseph's brothers went down to buy grain from Egypt.

Genesis 47:11
So Joseph settled his father and his brothers in Egypt and gave them property in the best part of the land, the district of Rameses, as Pharaoh directed.

Genesis 50:26
So Joseph died at the age of a hundred and ten. And after they embalmed him, he was placed in a coffin in Egypt.

Moses c.1200 Exodus 1:8
Then a new king, who did not know about Joseph, came to power in Egypt.

Exodus 2:5
Then Pharaoh's daughter went down to the Nile to bathe, and her attendants were walking along the river bank. She saw the basket among the reeds and sent her slave girl to get it.

Exodus 2:23
During that long period, the king of Egypt died. The Israelites groaned in their slavery and cried out, and their cry for help because of their slavery went up to God.

Exodus 3:10−12
'So now, go. I [God] am sending you to Pharaoh to bring my people the Israelites out of Egypt'. But Moses said to God, 'Who am I, that I should go to Pharaoh and bring the Israelites out of Egypt?' And God said, 'I will be with you. And this will be the sign to you that it is I who have sent you: When you have brought the people out of Egypt, you will worship God on this mountain.'

Exodus 6:13
Now the Lord spoke to Moses and Aaron about the Israelites and Pharaoh king of Egypt, and he commanded them to bring the Israelites out of Egypt.

Exodus 12:12−13
On that same night I will pass through Egypt and strike down every firstborn − both men and animals − and I will bring judgment on all the gods of Egypt. I am the Lord. The blood will be a sign for you on the houses where you are; and when I see the blood, I will pass over you. No destructive plague will touch you when I strike Egypt.

Exodus 14:5
When the king of Egypt was told that the people had fled, Pharaoh and his officials changed their minds about them and said, 'What have we done? We have let the Israelites go and have lost their services!'

Exodus 14:25
He made the wheels of their chariots come off [swerve] so that they had difficulty driving. And the Egyptians said, 'Let's get away from the Israelites! The Lord is fighting for them against Egypt.'

Hebrews 11:26−27
He [Moses] regarded disgrace for the sake of Christ as of greater value than the treasures of Egypt, because he was looking ahead to his reward. By faith he left Egypt, not fearing the king's anger; he persevered because he saw him who is invisible.

Solomon c.970−930 1 Kings 3:1
Solomon made an alliance with Pharaoh king of Egypt and married his daughter. He brought her to the City of David until he finished building his palace and the temple of the Lord, and the wall around Jerusalem.

2 Chronicles 1:16−17
Solomon's horses were imported from Egypt and from Kue − the royal merchants purchased them from Kue. They imported a chariot from Egypt for six hundred shekels of silver, and a horse for a hundred and fifty. They also exported them to all the kings of the Hittites and of the Arameans.

1 Kings 11:14,17−18,21
Then the Lord raised up against Solomon an adversary, Hadad, the Edomite, from the royal line of Edom. But Hadad, still only a boy, fled to Egypt with some Edomite officials who had served his father. They set out from Midian and went to Paran. Then taking men from Paran with them, they went to Egypt, to Pharaoh king of Egypt, who gave Hadad a house and land and provided him with food.   While he was in Egypt, Hadad heard that David rested with his fathers and that Joab the commander of the army was also dead. Then Hadad said to Pharaoh, 'Let me go, that I may return to my own country.'

Israel and Judah: the divided kingdom c.900−600 1 Kings 14:25
In the fifth year of King Rehoboam, Shishak king of Egypt attacked Jerusalem.

2 Chronicles 12:9
When Shishak king of Egypt attacked Jerusalem, he carried off the treasures of the temple of the Lord and the treasures of the royal palace. He took everything, including the gold shields Solomon had made.

2 Kings 18:21
Look now, you are depending on Egypt, that splintered reed of a staff, which pierces a man's hand and wounds him if he leans on it! Such is Pharaoh king of Egypt to all who depend on him.

2 Kings 23:29
While Josiah was king, Pharaoh Neco king of Egypt went up to help the king of Assyria by way of the Euphrates River. King Josiah marched out to meet him in battle, but Neco faced him and killed him at Megiddo.

2 Kings 24:7
The king of Egypt did not march out from his own country again, because the king of Babylon had taken all his territory, from the Wadi of Egypt to the Euphrates River.

Isaiah 19:1, 6−8
An oracle concerning Egypt:
    See, the Lord rides on a swift cloud and is coming to Egypt.

The idols of Egypt tremble before him,
and the hearts of the Egyptians melt within them.
The canals will stink; the streams of Egypt will dwindle and dry up.
The reeds and rushes will wither,
also the plants along the Nile, at the mouth of the river.
Every sown field along the Nile will become parched,
will blow away and be no more.
The fishermen will groan and lament, all who cast hooks into the Nile;
those who throw nets on the water will pine away.

Jeremiah 42:14-19
If you say, 'No, we will go and live in Egypt, where we will not see war or hear the trumpet or be hungry for bread,' then hear the word of the Lord, O remnant of Judah. This is what the Lord Almighty, the God of Israel, says: 'If you are determined to go to Egypt and you do go to settle there, then the sword you fear will overtake you there, and the famine you dread will follow you into Egypt, and there you will die. Indeed, all who are determined to go to Egypt to settle there will die by the sword, famine and plague; not one of them will survive or escape the disaster I will bring on them.' This is what the Lord Almighty, the God of Israel, says: 'As my anger and wrath have been poured out on those who lived in Jerusalem, so will my wrath be poured out on you when you go to Egypt. You will be an object of cursing and horror, of condemnation and reproach; you will never see this place again.' O remnant of Judah, the Lord has told you, 'Do not go to Egypt.' Be sure of this: I warn you today…

Jesus in Egypt Matthew 2:13-15
When they had gone, an angel of the Lord appeared to Joseph in a dream. 'Get up,' he said, 'take the child and his mother and escape to Egypt. Stay there until I tell you, for Herod is going to search for the child to kill him.' So he got up, took the child and his mother during the night and left for Egypt, where he stayed until the death of Herod. And so was fulfilled what the Lord had said through the prophet: 'Out of Egypt I called my son.'

Day of Pentecost Acts 2:10
Phrygia and Pamphylia, Egypt and the parts of Libya near Cyrene; visitors from Rome…
(*These quotations are a selection from the 439 references to Egypt in the Bible*)

Sinai and Horeb in the Bible

Moses c.1200 Exodus 3:1
Now Moses was tending the flock of Jethro his father-in-law, the priest of Midian, and he led the flock to the far side of the desert and came to Horeb, the mountain of God.

Acts 7:30
After forty years had passed, an angel appeared to Moses in the flames of a
burning bush in the desert near Mount Sinai.

Exodus 16:1
The whole Israelite community set out from Elim and came to the Desert of Sin,
which is between Elim and Sinai, on the fifteenth day of the second month after
they had come out of Egypt.

Exodus 17:6
'I [the Lord] will stand there before you by the rock at Horeb. Strike the rock,
and water will come out of it for the people to drink.' So Moses did this in the
sight of the elders of Israel.

Exodus 19:18
Mount Sinai was covered with smoke, because the Lord descended on it in fire.
The smoke billowed up from it like smoke from a furnace, the whole mountain
trembled violently, ...

Exodus 24:16
And the glory of the Lord settled on Mount Sinai. For six days the cloud covered
the mountain, and on the seventh day the Lord called to Moses from within the
cloud.

Exodus 31:18
When the Lord finished speaking to Moses on Mount Sinai, he gave him the two
tablets of the Testimony, the tablets of stone inscribed by the finger of God.

Exodus 34:29
When Moses came down from Mount Sinai with the two tablets of the
Testimony in his hands, he was not aware that his face was radiant because he
had spoken with the Lord.

Leviticus 26:46
These are the decrees, the laws and the regulations that the Lord established on
Mount Sinai between himself and the Israelites through Moses.

Elijah c.870–850 1 Kings 19:8
So he got up and ate and drank. Strengthened by that food, he travelled forty
days and forty nights until he reached Horeb, the mountain of God.
(These are some of the 55 references to Sinai/Horeb in the Bible.)

Edom in the Bible

Genesis 14:6
And the Horites in the hill country of Seir, as far as El Paran near the desert.

Jacob c.1800–1700 Genesis 25:30
He said to Jacob, 'Quick, let me have some of that red stew! I'm famished!'
(That is why he was also called Edom.)

Genesis 32:3
Jacob sent messengers ahead of him to his brother Esau in the land of Seir, the country of Edom.

Genesis 33:14
So let my lord [Esau] go on ahead of his servant, while I move along slowly at the pace of the droves before me and that of the children, until I come to my lord in Seir.

Genesis 33:16
So that day Esau started on his way back to Seir.

Genesis 36:1
This is the account of Esau (that is, Edom).

Genesis 36:8-9
So Esau (that is, Edom) settled in the hill country of Seir. This is the account of Esau the father of the Edomites in the hill country of Seir.

Genesis 36:16-17
Korah, Gatam and Amalek. These were the chiefs descended from Eliphaz in Edom; they were grandsons of Adah. The sons of Esau's son Reuel: Chiefs Nahath, Zerah, Shammah and Mizzah. These were the chiefs descended from Reuel in Edom; they were grandsons of Esau's wife Basemath.

Genesis 36:19-21
These were the sons of Esau (that is, Edom), and these were their chiefs. These were the sons of Seir the Horite, who were living in the region: Lotan, Shobal, Zibeon, Anah, Dishon, Ezer and Dishan. These sons of Seir in Edom were Horite chiefs. (See also I Chronicles 1:38)

Genesis 36:30-32
Dishon, Ezer and Dishan. These were the Horite chiefs, according to their divisions, in the land of Seir. These were the kings who reigned in Edom before any Israelite king reigned: Bela son of Beor became king of Edom. His city was named Dinhabah. (See also I Chronicles 1:43)

1 Chronicles 1:51
The chiefs of Edom were: Timna, Alvah, Jetheth,...

Genesis 36:43
Magdiel and Iram. These were the chiefs of Edom, according to their settlements in the land they occupied. This was Esau, the father of the Edomites. (See also I Chronicles 1:54)

Moses c.1200 Exodus 15:15
The chiefs of Edom will be terrified, the leaders of Moab will be seized with trembling, the people of Canaan will melt away;...

Numbers 20:14
Moses sent messengers from Kadesh to the king of Edom, saying: 'This is what your brother Israel says: You know about all the hardships that have come upon us.'

Numbers 20:18
But Edom answered: 'You may not pass through here; if you try, we will march out and attack you with the sword.'

Numbers 20:20−21
Again they answered: 'You may not pass through.' Then Edom came out against them with a large and powerful army. Since Edom refused to let them go through their territory, Israel turned away from them.

Judges 11:17−18
Then Israel sent messengers to the king of Edom, saying, 'Give us permission to go through your country,' but the king of Edom would not listen. They sent also to the king of Moab, and he refused. So Israel stayed at Kadesh. Next they travelled through the desert, skirted the lands of Edom and Moab, passed along the eastern side of the country of Moab, and camped on the other side of the Arnon. They did not enter the territory of Moab, for the Arnon was its border.

Numbers 20:23
At Mount Hor, near the border of Edom, the Lord said to Moses and Aaron, ...

Numbers 21:4
They travelled from Mount Hor along the route to the Red Sea, to go around Edom. But the people grew impatient on the way;...

Numbers 24:18
Edom will be conquered; Seir, his enemy, will be conquered, but Israel will grow strong.

Numbers 33:37
They left Kadesh and camped at Mount Hor, on the border of Edom.

Numbers 34:3
Your southern side will include some of the Desert of Zin along the border of Edom. On the east, your southern boundary will start from the end of the Salt Sea,...

Deuteronomy 1:2
It takes eleven days to go from Horeb to Kadesh Barnea by the Mount Seir road.

Deuteronomy 1:44
The Amorites who lived in those hills came out against you; they chased you like a swarm of bees and beat you down from Seir all the way to Hormah.

Deuteronomy 2:1
Then we turned back and set out toward the desert along the route to the Red Sea, as the Lord had directed me. For a long time we made our way around the hill country of Seir.

Deuteronomy 2:4–5
Give the people these orders: 'You are about to pass through the territory of your brothers the descendants of Esau, who live in Seir. They will be afraid of you, but be very careful. Do not provoke them to war, for I will not give you any of their land, not even enough to put your foot on. I have given Esau the hill country of Seir as his own.'

Deuteronomy 2:8
So we went on past our brothers the descendants of Esau, who live in Seir. We turned from the Arabah road, which comes up from Elath and Ezion Geber, and travelled along the desert road of Moab.

Deuteronomy 2:12
Horites used to live in Seir, but the descendants of Esau drove them out. They destroyed the Horites from before them and settled in their place, just as Israel did in the land the Lord gave them as their possession.

Deuteronomy 2:22
The Lord had done the same for the descendants of Esau, who lived in Seir, when he destroyed the Horites from before them. They drove them out and have lived in their place to this day.

Deuteronomy 2:29
As the descendants of Esau, who live in Seir, and the Moabites, who live in Ar, did for us – until we cross the Jordan into the land the Lord our God is giving us.

Deuteronomy 33:2
He [Moses] said: 'The Lord came from Sinai and dawned over them from Seir; he shone forth from Mount Paran. He came with myriads of holy ones from the south, from his mountain slopes.'

Joshua 1300–1190 Joshua 11:17
From Mount Halak, which rises toward Seir, to Baal Gad in the Valley of Lebanon below Mount Hermon. He captured all their kings and struck them down, putting them to death.

Joshua 12:7
These are the kings of the land that Joshua and the Israelites conquered on the west side of the Jordan, from Baal Gad in the Valley of Lebanon to Mount Halak, which rises toward Seir (their lands Joshua gave as an inheritance to the tribes of Israel according to their tribal divisions...

Joshua 15:1
The allotment for the tribe of Judah, clan by clan, extended down to the territory of Edom, to the Desert of Zin in the extreme south.

Joshua 15:10
Then it curved westward from Baalah to Mount Seir, ran along the northern slope of Mount Jearim (that is, Kesalon), continued down to Beth Shemesh and crossed to Timnah.

Joshua 15:21
The southernmost towns of the tribe of Judah in the Negev toward the boundary of Edom were: Kabzeel, Eder, Jagur,...

Joshua 24:4
And to Isaac I gave Jacob and Esau. I assigned the hill country of Seir to Esau, but Jacob and his sons went down to Egypt.

Judges 5:4
'O Lord, when you went out from Seir,
when you marched from the land of Edom, the earth shook,
the heavens poured, the clouds poured down water.'

Saul 1050–1011 1 Samuel 14:47
After Saul had assumed rule over Israel, he fought against their enemies on every side: Moab, the Ammonites, Edom, the kings of Zobah, and the Philistines. Wherever he turned, he inflicted punishment on them.

David 1011–970 2 Samuel 8:12
Edom and Moab, the Ammonites and the Philistines, and Amalek. He also dedicated the plunder taken from Hadadezer son of Rehob, king of Zobah.

1 Chronicles 18:11
King David dedicated these articles to the Lord, as he had done with the silver and gold he had taken from all these nations: Edom and Moab, the Ammonites and the Philistines, and Amalek.

2 Samuel 8:14
He put garrisons throughout Edom, and all the Edomites became subject to David. The Lord gave David victory wherever he went.
(See also 1 Chronicles 18:13)

Solomon 970–930 2 Chronicles 8:17
Then Solomon went to Ezion Geber and Elath on the coast of Edom.

1 Kings 9:26
King Solomon also built ships at Ezion Geber, which is near Elath in Edom, on the shore of the Red Sea.

1 Kings 11:14–16
Then the Lord raised up against Solomon an adversary, Hadad the Edomite, from the royal line of Edom. Earlier when David was fighting with Edom, Joab

the commander of the army, who had gone up to bury the dead, had struck down all the men in Edom. Joab and all the Israelites stayed there for six months, until they had destroyed all the men in Edom.

1 Kings 22:47
There was then no king in Edom; a deputy ruled.

Jehoshaphat 870–848 2 Chronicles 20:2
Some men came and told Jehoshaphat, 'A vast army is coming against you from Edom, from the other side of the Sea. It is already in Hazazon Tamar' (that is, En Gedi).

2 Chronicles 20:10
But now here are men from Ammon, Moab and Mount Seir, whose territory you would not allow Israel to invade when they came from Egypt; so they turned away from them and did not destroy them.

2 Chronicles 20:22–23
As they began to sing and praise, the Lord set ambushes against the men of Ammon and Moab and Mount Seir who were invading Judah, and they were defeated. The men of Ammon and Moab rose up against the men from Mount Seir to destroy and annihilate them. After they finished slaughtering the men from Seir, they helped to destroy one another.

Joram 852–841 Jehoshaphat 870–848 2 Kings 3:8–9
'By what route shall we attack?' he asked. 'Through the Desert of Edom', he answered. So the king of Israel set out with the king of Judah and the king of Edom. After a roundabout march of seven days, the army had no more water for themselves or for the animals with them.

2 Kings 3:12
Jehoshaphat said, 'The word of the Lord is with him.' So the king of Israel and Jehoshaphat and the king of Edom went down to him.

2 Kings 3:20
The next morning, about the time for offering the sacrifice, there it was – water flowing from the direction of Edom! And the land was filled with water.

2 Kings 3:26
When the king of Moab saw that the battle had gone against him, he took with him seven hundred swordsmen to break through to the king of Edom, but they failed.

Jehoram 852–841 2 Kings 8:20
In the time of Jehoram, Edom rebelled against Judah and set up its own king. (See also 2 Chronicles 21:8)

2 Chronicles 21:10
To this day Edom has been in rebellion against Judah. Libnah revolted at the same time, because Jehoram had forsaken the Lord, the God of his fathers.

Amaziah 796–767 2 Chronicles 25:11
Amaziah then marshalled his strength and led his army to the Valley of Salt, where he killed ten thousand men of Seir.

2 Chronicles 25:14
When Amaziah returned from slaughtering the Edomites, he brought back the gods of the people of Seir. He set them up as his own gods, bowed down to them and burned sacrifices to them.

2 Chronicles 25:19–20
You say to yourself that you have defeated Edom, and now you are arrogant and proud. But stay at home! Why ask for trouble and cause your own downfall and that of Judah also? Amaziah, however, would not listen, for God so worked that he might hand them over to Jehoash, because they sought the gods of Edom. (See also 2 Kings 14:10)

1 Chronicles 4:42
And five hundred of these Simeonites, led by Pelatiah, Neariah, Rephaiah and Uzziel, the sons of Ishi, invaded the hill country of Seir.

Psalm 60:8–9 & 108:9–10
    Moab is my washbasin, upon Edom I toss my sandal;
        over Philistia I shout in triumph.
    Who will bring me to the fortified city? Who will lead me to Edom?

Psalm 83:6
    The tents of Edom and the Ishmaelites, of Moab and the Hagrites,…

Isaiah 742–700   Isaiah 11:14
    They will swoop down on the slopes of Philistia to the west;
        together they will plunder the people to the east.
    They will lay hands on Edom and Moab,
        and the Ammonites will be subject to them.

Isaiah 21:11
    An oracle concerning Dumah: Someone calls to me from Seir,
    'Watchman, what is left of the night? Watchman, what is left of the night?'

Isaiah 34:5–6
    My sword has drunk its fill in the heavens;
        see, it descends in judgment on Edom, the people I have totally destroyed.
    The sword of the Lord is bathed in blood, it is covered with fat –
        the blood of lambs and goats, fat from the kidneys of rams.
    For the Lord has a sacrifice in Bozrah and a great slaughter in Edom.

Isaiah 34:11
    The desert owl and screech owl will possess it;
        the great owl and the raven will nest there.
    God will stretch out over Edom
        the measuring-line of chaos and the plumb-line of desolation.

Isaiah 63:1
Who is this coming from Edom,
from Bozrah, with his garments stained crimson?
Who is this, robed in splendour,
striding forward in the greatness of his strength?
'It is I, speaking in righteousness, mighty to save.'

Jeremiah 621–580 Jeremiah 9:26
Egypt, Judah, Edom, Ammon, Moab and all who live in the desert in distant places. For all these nations are really uncircumcised, and even the whole house of Israel is uncircumcised in heart.

Jeremiah 25:21
Edom, Moab and Ammon;...

Jeremiah 27:3
Then send word to the kings of Edom, Moab, Ammon, Tyre and Sidon through the envoys who have come to Jerusalem to Zedekiah king of Judah.

Jeremiah 40:11
When all the Jews in Moab, Ammon, Edom and all the other countries heard that the king of Babylon had left a remnant in Judah and had appointed Gedaliah son of Ahikam, the son of Shaphan, as governor over them,...

Jeremiah 49:7
Concerning Edom: This is what the Lord Almighty says:
'Is there no longer wisdom in Teman?
Has counsel perished from the prudent?   Has their wisdom decayed?'

Jeremiah 49:17
Edom will become an object of horror;
all who pass by will be appalled and will scoff because of all its wounds.

Jeremiah 49:19–20
Like a lion coming up from Jordan's thickets to a rich pasture-land,
I will chase Edom from its land in an instant.
Who is the chosen one I will appoint for this?
Who is like me and who can challenge me?
And what shepherd can stand against me?
Therefore, hear what the Lord has planned against Edom,
what he has purposed against those who live in Teman:
The young of the flock will be dragged away;
he will completely destroy their pasture because of them.

Lamentations 4:21–22
Rejoice and be glad, O Daughter of Edom, you who live in the land of Uz.
But to you also the cup will be passed; you will be drunk and stripped naked.
O Daughter of Zion, your punishment will end; he will not prolong your exile.

But, O Daughter of Edom, he will punish your sin and expose your wickedness.

Ezekiel 593–570   Ezekiel 16:57
...before your wickedness was uncovered. Even so, you are now scorned by the daughters of Edom and all her neighbours and the daughters of the Philistines – all those around you who despise you.

Ezekiel 25:8, 12–14
This is what the Sovereign Lord says: 'Because Moab and Seir said, "Look, the house of Judah has become like all the other nations," ...' This is what the Sovereign Lord says: 'Because Edom took revenge on the house of Judah and became very guilty by doing so', therefore this is what the Sovereign Lord says: 'I will stretch out my hand against Edom and kill its men and their animals. I will lay it waste, and from Teman to Dedan they will fall by the sword. I will take vengeance on Edom by the hand of my people Israel, and they will deal with Edom in accordance with my anger and my wrath; they will know my vengeance, declares the Sovereign Lord.'

Ezekiel 32:29
Edom is there, her kings and all her princes; despite their power, they are laid with those killed by the sword. They lie with the uncircumcised, with those who go down to the pit.

Ezekiel 35:2–3
Son of man, set your face against Mount Seir; prophesy against it and say: 'This is what the Sovereign Lord says: I am against you, Mount Seir, and I will stretch out my hand against you and make you a desolate waste'.

Ezekiel 35:7
I will make Mount Seir a desolate waste and cut off from it all who come and go.

Ezekiel 35:15
Because you rejoiced when the inheritance of the house of Israel became desolate, that is how I will treat you. You will be desolate, O Mount Seir, you and all of Edom. Then they will know that I am the Lord.

Ezekiel 36:5
This is what the Sovereign Lord says: In my burning zeal I have spoken against the rest of the nations, and against Edom, for with glee and with malice in their hearts they made my land their own possession so that they might plunder its pastureland.

Daniel 604–535   Daniel 11:41
He will also invade the Beautiful Land. Many countries will fall, but Edom, Moab and the leaders of Ammon will be delivered from his hand.

Joel 810–750   Joel 3:19
But Egypt will be desolate, Edom a desert waste, because of violence done to the people of Judah, in whose land they shed innocent blood.

Amos 760 Amos 1:6
This is what the Lord says:
'For three sins of Gaza, even for four, I will not turn back my wrath.
Because she took captive whole communities and sold them to Edom,'

Amos 1:9
This is what the Lord says:
'For three sins of Tyre, even for four, I will not turn back my wrath.
Because she sold whole communities of captives to Edom,
   disregarding a treaty of brotherhood,…'

Amos 1:11
This is what the Lord says:
'For three sins of Edom, even for four, I will not turn back my wrath.
Because he pursued his brother with a sword, stifling all compassion,
   because his anger raged continually and his fury flamed unchecked,…'

Amos 9:12
'…so that they may possess the remnant of Edom and all the nations that
   bear my name,' declares the Lord, who will do these things.

Obadiah 587 Obadiah 1:1
The vision of Obadiah. This is what the Sovereign Lord says about Edom –
We have heard a message from the Lord:
An envoy was sent to the nations to say,
'Rise, and let us go against her for battle…'

Obadiah 1:8
'In that day,' declares the Lord,
'will I not destroy the wise men of Edom
   men of understanding in the mountains of Esau?...'

Malachi c.460 Malachi 1:4
Edom may say, 'Though we have been crushed, we will rebuild the ruins.'   But
this is what the Lord Almighty says: 'They may build, but I will demolish. They
will be called the Wicked Land, a people always under the wrath of the Lord.'

Ezion Geber in the Bible

c.1200 Numbers 33:35–36
They left Abronah and camped at Ezion Geber.
They left Ezion Geber and camped at Kadesh, in the Desert of Zin.

Deuteronomy 2:8
So we went on past our brothers the descendants of Esau, who live in Seir. We
turned from the Arabah road, which comes up from Elath and Ezion Geber, and
travelled along the desert road of Moab.

Solomon 970–930 2 Chronicles 8:17
Then Solomon went to Ezion Geber and Elath on the coast of Edom.

1 Kings 9:26
King Solomon also built ships at Ezion Geber, which is near Elath in Edom, on the shore of the Red Sea.

Jehoshaphat 870–848 2 Chronicles 20:36
He agreed with him to construct a fleet of trading ships. After these were built at Ezion Geber,...

1 Kings 22:48
Now Jehoshaphat built a fleet of trading ships to go to Ophir for gold, but they never set sail – they were wrecked at Ezion Geber.

Moab in the Bible

c. 1800 Genesis 19:37
The older daughter had a son, and she named him Moab; he is the father of the Moabites of today.

Genesis 36:35
When Husham died, Hadad son of Bedad, who defeated Midian in the country of Moab, succeeded him as king. His city was named Avith.
(See also 1 Chronicles 1:46)

1 Chronicles 4:22
Jokim, the men of Cozeba, and Joash and Saraph, who ruled in Moab and Jashubi Lehem. (These records are from ancient times.)

1 Chronicles 8:8
Sons were born to Shaharaim in Moab after he had divorced his wives Hushim and Baara.

c.1260 Exodus 15:15
The chiefs of Edom will be terrified, the leaders of Moab will be seized with trembling, the people of Canaan will melt away;

c.1230 Numbers 21:11
Then they set out from Oboth and camped in Iye Abarim, in the desert that faces Moab toward the sunrise.

Numbers 21:13
They set out from there and camped alongside the Arnon, which is in the desert extending into Amorite territory. The Arnon is the border of Moab, between Moab and the Amorites.

Judges 11:17–18

Then Israel sent messengers to the king of Edom, saying, 'Give us permission to go through your country,' but the king of Edom would not listen. They sent also to the king of Moab, and he refused. So Israel stayed at Kadesh.   Next they travelled through the desert, skirted the lands of Edom and Moab, passed along the eastern side of the country of Moab, and camped on the other side of the Arnon. They did not enter the territory of Moab, for the Arnon was its border.

Numbers 21:15

And the slopes of the ravines that lead to the site of Ar and lie along the border of Moab.

Numbers 21:20

And from Bamoth to the valley in Moab where the top of Pisgah overlooks the wasteland.

Numbers 21:26

Heshbon was the city of Sihon king of the Amorites, who had fought against the former king of Moab and had taken from him all his land as far as the Arnon.

Numbers 21:28–29

Fire went out from Heshbon, a blaze from the city of Sihon.
It consumed Ar of Moab, the citizens of Arnon's heights.
Woe to you, O Moab! You are destroyed, O people of Chemosh!
He has given up his sons as fugitives
    and his daughters as captives to Sihon king of the Amorites.

Numbers 22:1

Then the Israelites travelled to the plains of Moab and camped along the Jordan across from Jericho.

Numbers 22:3–4

And Moab was terrified because there were so many people. Indeed, Moab was filled with dread because of the Israelites. The Moabites said to the elders of Midian, 'This horde is going to lick up everything around us, as an ox licks up the grass of the field.' So Balak son of Zippor, who was king of Moab at that time, ...

Numbers 22:7

The elders of Moab and Midian left, taking with them the fee for divination. When they came to Balaam, they told him what Balak had said.

Numbers 22:10

Balaam said to God, 'Balak son of Zippor, king of Moab, sent me this message:...'

Numbers 22:21
Balaam got up in the morning, saddled his donkey and went with the princes of Moab.

Numbers 23:6–7
So he went back to him and found him standing beside his offering, with all the princes of Moab. Then Balaam uttered his oracle:
'Balak brought me from Aram, the king of Moab from the eastern mountains. "Come," he said, "curse Jacob for me; come, denounce Israel."...'

Numbers 23:17
So he went to him and found him standing beside his offering, with the princes of Moab. Balak asked him, 'What did the Lord say?'

Numbers 24:17
I see him, but not now; I behold him, but not near.
A star will come out of Jacob; a sceptre will rise out of Israel.
He will crush the foreheads of Moab, the skulls of all the sons of Sheth.

Numbers 26:3
So on the plains of Moab by the Jordan across from Jericho, Moses and Eleazar the priest spoke with them and said, ...

Numbers 26:63
These are the ones counted by Moses and Eleazar the priest when they counted the Israelites on the plains of Moab by the Jordan across from Jericho.

Numbers 31:12
... and brought the captives, spoils and plunder to Moses and Eleazar the priest and the Israelite assembly at their camp on the plains of Moab, by the Jordan across from Jericho.

Numbers 33:44
They left Oboth and camped at Iye Abarim, on the border of Moab.

Numbers 33:48–50
They left the mountains of Abarim and camped on the plains of Moab by the Jordan across from Jericho. There on the plains of Moab they camped along the Jordan from Beth Jeshimoth to Abel Shittim. On the plains of Moab by the Jordan across from Jericho the Lord said to Moses,

Numbers 35:1
On the plains of Moab by the Jordan across from Jericho, the Lord said to Moses, ...

Numbers 36:13
These are the commands and regulations the Lord gave through Moses to the Israelites on the plains of Moab by the Jordan across from Jericho.

Deuteronomy 1:5
East of the Jordan in the territory of Moab, Moses began to expound this law, saying:...

Deuteronomy 2:8
So we went on past our brothers the descendants of Esau, who live in Seir. We turned from the Arabah road, which comes up from Elath and Ezion Geber, and travelled along the desert road of Moab.

Deuteronomy 2:18
Today you are to pass by the region of Moab at Ar.

Deuteronomy 29:1
These are the terms of the covenant the Lord commanded Moses to make with the Israelites in Moab, in addition to the covenant he had made with them at Horeb.

Deuteronomy 32:49
Go up into the Abarim Range to Mount Nebo in Moab, across from Jericho, and view Canaan, the land I am giving the Israelites as their own possession.

c.1230 Deuteronomy 34:1
Then Moses climbed Mount Nebo from the plains of Moab to the top of Pisgah, across from Jericho. There the Lord showed him the whole land − from Gilead to Dan,

Deuteronomy 34:5−6
And Moses the servant of the Lord died there in Moab, as the Lord had said. He buried him in Moab, in the valley opposite Beth Peor, but to this day no one knows where his grave is.

Deuteronomy 34:8
The Israelites grieved for Moses in the plains of Moab thirty days, until the time of weeping and mourning was over.

Joshua 13:32
This is the inheritance Moses had given when he was in the plains of Moab across the Jordan east of Jericho.

Joshua 24:9
When Balak son of Zippor, the king of Moab, prepared to fight against Israel, he sent for Balaam son of Beor to put a curse on you.

c.1150 Judges 3:12
Once again the Israelites did evil in the eyes of the Lord, and because they did this evil the Lord gave Eglon king of Moab power over Israel.

Judges 3:14−15
The Israelites were subject to Eglon king of Moab for eighteen years.

Again the Israelites cried out to the Lord, and he gave them a deliverer – Ehud, a left-handed man, the son of Gera the Benjamite. The Israelites sent him with tribute to Eglon king of Moab.

Judges 3:17
He presented the tribute to Eglon king of Moab, who was a very fat man.

Judges 3:28
'Follow me,' he ordered, 'for the Lord has given Moab, your enemy, into your hands.' So they followed him down and, taking possession of the fords of the Jordan that led to Moab, they allowed no one to cross over.

Judges 3:30
That day Moab was made subject to Israel, and the land had peace for eighty years.

Judges 10:6
Again the Israelites did evil in the eyes of the Lord. They served the Baals and the Ashtoreths, and the gods of Aram, the gods of Sidon, the gods of Moab, the gods of the Ammonites and the gods of the Philistines. And because the Israelites forsook the Lord and no longer served him,...

Judges 11:15
... saying: 'This is what Jephthah says: Israel did not take the land of Moab or the land of the Ammonites'.

Judges 11:25
Are you better than Balak son of Zippor, king of Moab? Did he ever quarrel with Israel or fight with them?

c.1180 Ruth 1:1–2
In the days when the judges ruled, there was a famine in the land, and a man from Bethlehem in Judah, together with his wife and two sons, went to live for a while in the country of Moab. The man's name was Elimelech, his wife's name Naomi, and the names of his two sons were Mahlon and Kilion. They were Ephrathites from Bethlehem, Judah. And they went to Moab and lived there.

Ruth 1:6
When she heard in Moab that the Lord had come to the aid of his people by providing food for them, Naomi and her daughters-in-law prepared to return home from there.

Ruth 1:22
So Naomi returned from Moab accompanied by Ruth the Moabitess, her daughter-in-law, arriving in Bethlehem as the barley harvest was beginning.

Ruth 2:6
The foreman replied, 'She is the Moabitess who came back from Moab with Naomi.'

Ruth 4:3
Then he said to the kinsman-redeemer, 'Naomi, who has come back from Moab, is selling the piece of land that belonged to our brother Elimelech....'

1 Samuel 12:9
But they forgot the Lord their God; so he sold them into the hand of Sisera, the commander of the army of Hazor, and into the hands of the Philistines and the king of Moab, who fought against them.

Saul 1050–1011 1 Samuel 14:47
After Saul had assumed rule over Israel, he fought against their enemies on every side: Moab, the Ammonites, Edom, the kings of Zobah, and the Philistines. Wherever he turned, he inflicted punishment on them.

David 1011–970 1 Samuel 22:3–4
From there David went to Mizpah in Moab and said to the king of Moab, 'Would you let my father and mother come and stay with you until I learn what God will do for me?' So he left them with the king of Moab, and they stayed with him as long as David was in the stronghold.

2 Samuel 8:12
Edom and Moab, the Ammonites and the Philistines, and Amalek. He also dedicated the plunder taken from Hadadezer son of Rehob, king of Zobah.

1 Chronicles 18:11
King David dedicated these articles to the Lord, as he had done with the silver and gold he had taken from all these nations: Edom and Moab, the Ammonites and the Philistines, and Amalek.

Solomon 970–930 1 Kings 11:7
On a hill east of Jerusalem, Solomon built a high place for Chemosh the detestable god of Moab, and for Molech the detestable god of the Ammonites.

2 Kings 1:1
After Ahab's death, Moab rebelled against Israel.

2 Kings 3:4–5
Now Mesha king of Moab raised sheep, and he had to supply the king of Israel with a hundred thousand lambs and with the wool of a hundred thousand rams. But after Ahab died, the king of Moab rebelled against the king of Israel.

2 Kings 3:7
He also sent this message to Jehoshaphat king of Judah: 'The king of Moab has rebelled against me. Will you go with me to fight against Moab?' 'I will go with

you,' he replied. 'I am as you are, my people as your people, my horses as your horses.'

2 Kings 3:10
'What!' exclaimed the king of Israel. 'Has the Lord called us three kings together only to hand us over to Moab?'

2 Kings 3:13
Elisha said to the king of Israel, 'What do we have to do with each other? Go to the prophets of your father and the prophets of your mother.' 'No,' the king of Israel answered, 'because it was the Lord who called us three kings together to hand us over to Moab.'

2 Kings 3:18
This is an easy thing in the eyes of the Lord; he will also hand Moab over to you.

2 Kings 3:23
'That's blood!' they said. 'Those kings must have fought and slaughtered each other. Now to the plunder, Moab!'

2 Kings 3:26
When the king of Moab saw that the battle had gone against him, he took with him seven hundred swordsmen to break through to the king of Edom, but they failed.

2 Chronicles 20:10
But now here are men from Ammon, Moab and Mount Seir, whose territory you would not allow Israel to invade when they came from Egypt; so they turned away from them and did not destroy them.

2 Chronicles 20:22–23
As they began to sing and praise, the Lord set ambushes against the men of Ammon and Moab and Mount Seir who were invading Judah, and they were defeated. The men of Ammon and Moab rose up against the men from Mount Seir to destroy and annihilate them. After they finished slaughtering the men from Seir, they helped to destroy one another.

Josiah 640–609 2 Kings 23:13
The king also desecrated the high places that were east of Jerusalem on the south of the Hill of Corruption – the ones Solomon king of Israel had built for Ashtoreth the vile goddess of the Sidonians, for Chemosh the vile god of Moab, and for Molech the detestable god of the people of Ammon.

Nehemiah 445–433 Nehemiah 13:23
Moreover, in those days I saw men of Judah who had married women from Ashdod, Ammon and Moab.

Psalm 60:8 & 108:9
Moab is my washbasin, upon Edom I toss my sandal;
over Philistia I shout in triumph.

Psalm 83:6
the tents of Edom and the Ishmaelites, of Moab and the Hagrites,

Isaiah 742–700   Isaiah 11:14
They will swoop down on the slopes of Philistia to the west;
together they will plunder the people to the east.
They will lay hands on Edom and Moab,
and the Ammonites will be subject to them.

Isaiah 15:1–2
An oracle concerning Moab: Ar in Moab is ruined, destroyed in a night!
Kir in Moab is ruined, destroyed in a night!
Dibon goes up to its temple, to its high places to weep;
Moab wails over Nebo and Medeba.
Every head is shaved and every beard cut off.

Isaiah 15:4–5
Heshbon and Elealeh cry out, their voices are heard all the way to Jahaz.
Therefore the armed men of Moab cry out, and their hearts are faint.
My heart cries out over Moab; her fugitives flee as far as Zoar,
as far as Eglath Shelishiyah.
They go up the way to Luhith, weeping as they go;
on the road to Horonaim they lament their destruction.

Isaiah 15:8–9
Their outcry echoes along the border of Moab;
their wailing reaches as far as Eglaim, their lamentation as far as Beer Elim.
Dimon's waters are full of blood, but I will bring still more upon Dimon –
a lion upon the fugitives of Moab and upon those who remain in the land.

Isaiah 16:2
Like fluttering birds pushed from the nest,
so are the women of Moab at the fords of the Arnon.

Isaiah 16:7
Therefore the Moabites wail, they wail together for Moab.
Lament and grieve for the men of Kir Hareseth.

Isaiah 16:11–13
My heart laments for Moab like a harp, my inmost being for Kir Hareseth.
When Moab appears at her high place, she only wears herself out;
when she goes to her shrine to pray,   it is to no avail.
This is the word the Lord has already spoken concerning Moab.

Isaiah 25:10
The hand of the Lord will rest on this mountain; but Moab will be trampled under him as straw is trampled down in the manure.

Jeremiah 621−580 Jeremiah 9:26
Egypt, Judah, Edom, Ammon, Moab and all who live in the desert in distant places. For all these nations are really uncircumcised, and even the whole house of Israel is uncircumcised in heart.

Jeremiah 25:21
Edom, Moab and Ammon;…

Jeremiah 27:3
Then send word to the kings of Edom, Moab, Ammon, Tyre and Sidon through the envoys who have come to Jerusalem to Zedekiah king of Judah.

Jeremiah 40:11
When all the Jews in Moab, Ammon, Edom and all the other countries heard that the king of Babylon had left a remnant in Judah and had appointed Gedaliah son of Ahikam, the son of Shaphan, as governor over them,…

Jeremiah 48:1−2
Concerning Moab: This is what the Lord Almighty, the God of Israel, says:
 'Woe to Nebo, for it will be ruined.Kiriathaim will be disgraced and captured;
  the stronghold will be disgraced and shattered.
 Moab will be praised no more; in Heshbon men will plot her downfall:
  "Come, let us put an end to that nation."
 You too, O Madmen, will be silenced; the sword will pursue you.'

Jeremiah 48:4
 Moab will be broken; her little ones will cry out.

Jeremiah 48:9
 Put salt on Moab, for she will be laid waste;
 her towns will become desolate, with no one to live in them.

Jeremiah 48:11
 Moab has been at rest from youth, like wine left on its dregs,
 not poured from one jar to another − she has not gone into exile.
 So she tastes as she did, and her aroma is unchanged.

Jeremiah 48:13
 Then Moab will be ashamed of Chemosh,
  as the house of Israel was ashamed when they trusted in Bethel.

Jeremiah 48:15−16
 Moab will be destroyed and her towns invaded;
 her finest young men will go down in the slaughter,

declares the King, whose name is the Lord Almighty.
The fall of Moab is at hand; her calamity will come quickly.

Jeremiah 48:18
Come down from your glory and sit on the parched ground,
O inhabitants of the Daughter of Dibon,
for he who destroys Moab will come up against you
and ruin your fortified cities.

Jeremiah 48:20
Moab is disgraced, for she is shattered. Wail and cry out!
Announce by the Arnon that Moab is destroyed.

Jeremiah 48:24
To Kerioth and Bozrah to all the towns of Moab, far and near.

Jeremiah 48:26
Make her drunk, for she has defied the Lord.
Let Moab wallow in her vomit; let her be an object of ridicule.

Jeremiah 48:28
Abandon your towns and dwell among the rocks, you who live in Moab.
Be like a dove that makes its nest at the mouth of a cave.

Jeremiah 48:31
Therefore I wail over Moab, for all Moab I cry out,
I moan for the men of Kir Hareseth.

Jeremiah 48:33
Joy and gladness are gone from the orchards and fields of Moab.
I have stopped the flow of wine from the presses;
no one treads them with shouts of joy.
Although there are shouts, they are not shouts of joy.

Jeremiah 48:35–36
In Moab I will put an end to those who make offerings on the high places
and burn incense to their gods, declares the Lord.
So my heart laments for Moab like a flute;
it laments like a flute for the men of Kir Hareseth.
The wealth they acquired is gone.

Jeremiah 48:38–40
On all the roofs in Moab and in the public squares
there is nothing but mourning,
for I have broken Moab like a jar that no one wants, declares the Lord.
How shattered she is! How they wail! How Moab turns her back in shame!
Moab has become an object of ridicule,
an object of horror to all those around her.

This is what the Lord says:
'Look! An eagle is swooping down, spreading its wings over Moab.'

Jeremiah 48:42–47
Moab will be destroyed as a nation because she defied the Lord.
Terror and pit and snare await you, O people of Moab, declares the Lord.
Whoever flees from the terror will fall into a pit,
whoever climbs out of the pit will be caught in a snare;
for I will bring upon Moab the year of her punishment, declares the Lord.
In the shadow of Heshbon the fugitives stand helpless,
for a fire has gone out from Heshbon, a blaze from the midst of Sihon;
it burns the foreheads of Moab, the skulls of the noisy boasters.
Woe to you, O Moab! The people of Chemosh are destroyed;
your sons are taken into exile and your daughters into captivity.
Yet I will restore the fortunes of Moab in days to come, declares the Lord.
Here ends the judgment on Moab.

Ezekiel 593–570 Ezekiel 25:8–11
This is what the Sovereign Lord says: 'Because Moab and Seir said, "Look, the house of Judah has become like all the other nations," therefore I will expose the flank of Moab, beginning at its frontier towns – Beth Jeshimoth, Baal Meon and Kiriathaim – the glory of that land. I will give Moab along with the Ammonites to the people of the East as a possession, so that the Ammonites will not be remembered among the nations; and I will inflict punishment on Moab. Then they will know that I am the Lord.'

Daniel 604–535 Daniel 11:41
He will also invade the Beautiful Land. Many countries will fall, but Edom, Moab and the leaders of Ammon will be delivered from his hand.

Amos c.760 Amos 2:1–2
This is what the Lord says:
For three sins of Moab, even for four, I will not turn back my wrath.
Because he burned, as if to lime, the bones of Edom's king,
I will send fire upon Moab that will consume the fortresses of Kerioth.
Moab will go down in great tumult amid war cries
and the blast of the trumpet.

Micah 742–687 Micah 6:5
My people, remember what Balak king of Moab counselled
and what Balaam son of Beor answered.
Remember your journey from Shittim to Gilgal,
that you may know the righteous acts of the Lord.

Zephaniah 640   Zephaniah 2:8–9
'I have heard the insults of Moab and the taunts of the Ammonites,
who insulted my people and made threats against their land.
Therefore, as surely as I live,' declares the Lord Almighty, the God of Israel,
'surely Moab will become like Sodom, the Ammonites like Gomorrah –
a place of weeds and salt pits, a wasteland forever.
The remnant of my people will plunder them;
    the survivors of my nation will inherit their land.'

Ammon in the Bible

Genesis 19:38
The younger daughter also had a son, and she named him Ben-Ammi; he is the father of the Ammonites of today.

c.1230   Numbers 21:24
Israel, however, put him to the sword and took over his land from the Arnon to the Jabbok, but only as far as the Ammonites, because their border was fortified.

Deuteronomy 2:19–21
When you come to the Ammonites, do not harass them or provoke them to war, for I will not give you possession of any land belonging to the Ammonites. I have given it as a possession to the descendants of Lot. That too was considered a land of the Rephaites, who used to live there; but the Ammonites called them Zamzummites. They were a people strong and numerous, and as tall as the Anakites. The Lord destroyed them from before the Ammonites, who drove them out and settled in their place...

Deuteronomy 2:37
But in accordance with the command of the Lord our God, you did not encroach on any of the land of the Ammonites, neither the land along the course of the Jabbok nor that around the towns in the hills.

Deuteronomy 3:11
Only Og king of Bashan was left of the remnant of the Rephaites. His bed was made of iron and was more than thirteen feet long and six feet wide. It is still in Rabbah of the Ammonites.

Deuteronomy 3:16
But to the Reubenites and the Gadites I gave the territory extending from Gilead down to the Arnon Gorge (the middle of the gorge being the border) and out to the Jabbok River, which is the border of the Ammonites.

Joshua 12:2
Sihon king of the Amorites, who reigned in Heshbon. He ruled from Aroer on the rim of the Arnon Gorge – from the middle of the gorge – to the Jabbok River, which is the border of the Ammonites. This included half of Gilead.

Joshua 13:10
And all the towns of Sihon king of the Amorites, who ruled in Heshbon, out to the border of the Ammonites.

Judges c.1150 Judges 3:13
Getting the Ammonites and Amalekites to join him, Eglon came and attacked Israel, and they took possession of the City of Palms.

Judges 10:67
Again the Israelites did evil in the eyes of the Lord. They served the Baals and the Ashtoreths, and the gods of Aram, the gods of Sidon, the gods of Moab, the gods of the Ammonites and the gods of the Philistines. And because the Israelites forsook the Lord and no longer served him, he became angry with them. He sold them into the hands of the Philistines and the Ammonites.

Judges 10:9
The Ammonites also crossed the Jordan to fight against Judah, Benjamin and the house of Ephraim; and Israel was in great distress.

Judges 10:11
The Lord replied, 'When the Egyptians, the Amorites, the Ammonites, the Philistines,...'

Judges 10:17-18
When the Ammonites were called to arms and camped in Gilead, the Israelites assembled and camped at Mizpah. The leaders of the people of Gilead said to each other, 'Whoever will launch the attack against the Ammonites will be the head of all those living in Gilead.'

Judges 11:4
Some time later, when the Ammonites made war on Israel,...

Judges 11:6
'Come,' they said, 'be our commander, so we can fight the Ammonites.'

Judges 11:8-9
The elders of Gilead said to him, 'Nevertheless, we are turning to you now; come with us to fight the Ammonites, and you will be our head over all who live in Gilead.' Jephthah answered, 'Suppose you take me back to fight the Ammonites and the Lord gives them to me – will I really be your head?'

Judges 11:13
The king of the Ammonites answered Jephthah's messengers, 'When Israel came up out of Egypt, they took away my land from the Arnon to the Jabbok, all the way to the Jordan. Now give it back peaceably.'

Judges 11:15
'This is what Jephthah says: Israel did not take the land of Moab or the land of the Ammonites.'

Judges 11:27–33
I have not wronged you, but you are doing me wrong by waging war against me. Let the Lord, the Judge, decide the dispute this day between the Israelites and the Ammonites. The king of Ammon, however, paid no attention to the message Jephthah sent him. Then the Spirit of the Lord came upon Jephthah. He crossed Gilead and Manasseh, passed through Mizpah of Gilead, and from there he advanced against the Ammonites. And Jephthah made a vow to the Lord: 'If you give the Ammonites into my hands, whatever comes out of the door of my house to meet me when I return in triumph from the Ammonites will be the Lord's, and I will sacrifice it as a burnt offering.' Then Jephthah went over to fight the Ammonites, and the Lord gave them into his hands. He devastated twenty towns from Aroer to the vicinity of Minnith, as far as Abel Keramim. Thus Israel subdued Ammon.

Judges 11:36
'My father,' she replied, 'you have given your word to the Lord. Do to me just as you promised, now that the Lord has avenged you of your enemies, the Ammonites.'

Judges 12:1–3
The men of Ephraim called out their forces, crossed over to Zaphon and said to Jephthah, 'Why did you go to fight the Ammonites without calling us to go with you? We're going to burn down your house over your head.'
Jephthah answered, 'I and my people were engaged in a great struggle with the Ammonites, and although I called, you didn't save me out of their hands. When I saw that you wouldn't help, I took my life in my hands and crossed over to fight the Ammonites, and the Lord gave me the victory over them. Now why have you come up today to fight me?'

Saul 1050–1011 1 Samuel 11:10–11
They said to the Ammonites, 'Tomorrow we will surrender to you, and you can do to us whatever seems good to you.' The next day Saul separated his men into three divisions; during the last watch of the night they broke into the camp of the Ammonites and slaughtered them until the heat of the day. Those who survived were scattered, so that no two of them were left together.

1 Samuel 12:12
But when you saw that Nahash king of the Ammonites was moving against you, you said to me, 'No, we want a king to rule over us' – even though the Lord your God was your king.

1 Samuel 14:47
After Saul had assumed rule over Israel, he fought against their enemies on every side: Moab, the Ammonites, Edom, the kings of Zobah, and the Philistines. Wherever he turned, he inflicted punishment on them.

David 1011−970 2 Samuel 8:12
Edom and Moab, the Ammonites and the Philistines, and Amalek. He also dedicated the plunder taken from Hadadezer son of Rehob, king of Zobah.

1 Chronicles 18:11
King David dedicated these articles to the Lord, as he had done with the silver and gold he had taken from all these nations: Edom and Moab, the Ammonites and the Philistines, and Amalek.

2 Samuel 10:1−2
In the course of time, the king of the Ammonites died, and his son Hanun succeeded him as king. David thought, 'I will show kindness to Hanun son of Nahash, just as his father showed kindness to me.' So David sent a delegation to express his sympathy to Hanun concerning his father. When David's men came to the land of the Ammonites,...   (See also 1 Chronicles 19:1−2)

2 Samuel 10:6
When the Ammonites realized that they had become a stench in David's nostrils, they hired twenty thousand Aramean foot soldiers from Beth Rehob and Zobah, as well as the king of Maacah with a thousand men, and also twelve thousand men from Tob. (See also 1 Chronicles 19:6−7)

2 Samuel 10:8
The Ammonites came out and drew up in battle formation at the entrance to their city gate, while the Arameans of Zobah and Rehob and the men of Tob and Maacah were by themselves in the open country. (See also 1 Chronicles 19:9)

2 Samuel 10:10−11
He put the rest of the men under the command of Abishai his brother and deployed them against the Ammonites. Joab said, 'If the Arameans are too strong for me, then you are to come to my rescue; but if the Ammonites are too strong for you, then I will come to rescue you'.
(See also 1 Chronicles 19:11−12)

2 Samuel 10:14
When the Ammonites saw that the Arameans were fleeing, they fled before Abishai and went inside the city. So Joab returned from fighting the Ammonites and came to Jerusalem. (See also 1 Chronicles 19:15)

2 Samuel 10:19−11:1
When all the kings who were vassals of Hadadezer saw that they had been defeated by Israel, they made peace with the Israelites and became subject to them. So the Arameans were afraid to help the Ammonites anymore.

In the spring, at the time when kings go off to war, David sent Joab out with the king's men and the whole Israelite army. They destroyed the Ammonites and besieged Rabbah. But David remained in Jerusalem.
(See also 1 Chronicles 19:19−20:1)

2 Samuel 12:9
Why did you despise the word of the Lord by doing what is evil in his eyes? You struck down Uriah the Hittite with the sword and took his wife to be your own. You killed him with the sword of the Ammonites.

2 Samuel 12:26
Meanwhile Joab fought against Rabbah of the Ammonites and captured the royal citadel.

2 Samuel 17:27
When David came to Mahanaim, Shobi son of Nahash from Rabbah of the Ammonites, and Makir son of Ammiel from Lo Debar, and Barzillai the Gileadite from Rogelim

Soloman 970−930   1 Kings 11:1
King Solomon, however, loved many foreign women besides Pharaoh's daughter − Moabites, Ammonites, Edomites, Sidonians and Hittites.

1 Kings 11:5
He followed Ashtoreth the goddess of the Sidonians, and Molech the detestable god of the Ammonites.

1 Kings 11:7
On a hill east of Jerusalem, Solomon built a high place for Chemosh the detestable god of Moab, and for Molech the detestable god of the Ammonites.

1 Kings 11:33
I will do this because they have forsaken me and worshiped Ashtoreth the goddess of the Sidonians, Chemosh the god of the Moabites, and Molech the god of the Ammonites, and have not walked in my ways, nor done what is right in my eyes, nor kept my statutes and laws as David, Solomon's father, did.

Jehoshaphat 870−848   2 Chronicles 20:1
After this, the Moabites and Ammonites with some of the Meunites came to make war on Jehoshaphat.

2 Chronicles 20:10
But now here are men from Ammon, Moab and Mount Seir, whose territory you would not allow Israel to invade when they came from Egypt; so they turned away from them and did not destroy them.

2 Chronicles 20:22−23
As they began to sing and praise, the Lord set ambushes against the men of Ammon and Moab and Mount Seir who were invading Judah, and they were

defeated. The men of Ammon and Moab rose up against the men from Mount Seir to destroy and annihilate them. After they finished slaughtering the men from Seir, they helped to destroy one another.

Uzziah 767–740   2 Chronicles 26:8
The Ammonites brought tribute to Uzziah, and his fame spread as far as the border of Egypt, because he had become very powerful.

Jotham 740–732   2 Chronicles 27:5
Jotham made war on the king of the Ammonites and conquered them. That year the Ammonites paid him a hundred talents of silver, ten thousand cors of wheat and ten thousand cors of barley. The Ammonites brought him the same amount also in the second and third years.

Josiah 640–609   2 Kings 23:13
Josiah also desecrated the high places that were east of Jerusalem on the south of the Hill of Corruption – the ones Solomon king of Israel had built for Ashtoreth the vile goddess of the Sidonians, for Chemosh the vile god of Moab, and for Molech the detestable god of the people of Ammon.

Ezra c.458   Ezra 9:1
After these things had been done, the leaders came to me and said, 'The people of Israel, including the priests and the Levites, have not kept themselves separate from the neighbouring peoples with their detestable practices, like those of the Canaanites, Hittites, Perizzites, Jebusites, Ammonites, Moabites, Egyptians and Amorites'.

Nehemiah 445–433   Nehemiah 4:7
But when Sanballat, Tobiah, the Arabs, the Ammonites and the men of Ashdod heard that the repairs to Jerusalem's walls had gone ahead and that the gaps were being closed, they were very angry.

Nehemiah 13:23
Moreover, in those days I saw men of Judah who had married women from Ashdod, Ammon and Moab.

Psalm 83:7
Gebal, Ammon and Amalek, Philistia, with the people of Tyre.

Isaiah 742–700   Isaiah 11:14
They will swoop down on the slopes of Philistia to the west;
   together they will plunder the people to the east.
They will lay hands on Edom and Moab,
   and the Ammonites will be subject to them.

Jeremiah 621–580 Jeremiah 9:26
Egypt, Judah, Edom, Ammon, Moab and all who live in the desert in distant places. For all these nations are really uncircumcised, and even the whole house of Israel is uncircumcised in heart.

Jeremiah 25:21
Edom, Moab and Ammon;...

Jeremiah 27:3
Then send word to the kings of Edom, Moab, Ammon, Tyre and Sidon through the envoys who have come to Jerusalem to Zedekiah king of Judah.

Jeremiah 40:11
When all the Jews in Moab, Ammon, Edom and all the other countries heard that the king of Babylon had left a remnant in Judah and had appointed Gedaliah son of Ahikam, the son of Shaphan, as governor over them,

Jeremiah 40:14
And said to him, 'Don't you know that Baalis king of the Ammonites has sent Ishmael son of Nethaniah to take your life?' But Gedaliah son of Ahikam did not believe them.

Jeremiah 41:10
Ishmael made captives of all the rest of the people who were in Mizpah – the king's daughters along with all the others who were left there, over whom Nebuzaradan commander of the imperial guard had appointed Gedaliah son of Ahikam. Ishmael son of Nethaniah took them captive and set out to cross over to the Ammonites.

Jeremiah 41:15
But Ishmael son of Nethaniah and eight of his men escaped from Johanan and fled to the Ammonites.

Jeremiah 49:1–2
Concerning the Ammonites: This is what the Lord says:
   'Has Israel no sons? Has she no heirs?
   Why then has Molech taken possession of Gad?
   Why do his people live in its towns? '
   'But the days are coming,' declares the Lord,
      'when I will sound the battle cry against Rabbah of the Ammonites;
      it will become a mound of ruins,
      and its surrounding villages will be set on fire.
   Then Israel will drive out those who drove her out,' says the Lord.

Jeremiah 49:6
'Yet afterward, I will restore the fortunes of the Ammonites,' declares the Lord.

Ezekiel 593–570 Ezekiel 21:20
Mark out one road for the sword to come against Rabbah of the Ammonites and another against Judah and fortified Jerusalem.

Ezekiel 21:28
And you, son of man, prophesy and say, this is what the Sovereign Lord says about the Ammonites and their insults:
'A sword, a sword, drawn for the slaughter,
    polished to consume and to flash like lightning!'

Ezekiel 25:2
Son of man, set your face against the Ammonites and prophesy against them.

Ezekiel 25:5
I will turn Rabbah into a pasture for camels and Ammon into a resting place for sheep. Then you will know that I am the Lord.

Ezekiel 25:10
I will give Moab along with the Ammonites to the people of the East as a possession, so that the Ammonites will not be remembered among the nations;

Daniel 604–535 Daniel 11:41
He will also invade the Beautiful Land. Many countries will fall, but Edom, Moab and the leaders of Ammon will be delivered from his hand.

Amos 760 Amos 1:13
This is what the Lord says:
'For three sins of Ammon, even for four,
I will not turn back my wrath.
Because he ripped open the pregnant women of Gilead
    in order to extend his borders,

Zephaniah c.640 Zephaniah 2:8–9
'I have heard the insults of Moab and the taunts of the Ammonites,
    who insulted my people and made threats against their land.
Therefore, as surely as I live,'
    declares the Lord Almighty, the God of Israel,
'surely Moab will become like Sodom, the Ammonites like Gomorrah –
    a place of weeds and salt pits, a wasteland forever.
The remnant of my people will plunder them;
    the survivors of my nation will inherit their land.'

Amorite in the Bible

c.1900 Genesis 14:13
One who had escaped came and reported this to Abram the Hebrew. Now Abram was living near the great trees of Mamre the Amorite, a brother of Eshcol and Aner, all of whom were allied with Abram.

c.1230 Numbers 21:13
They set out from there and camped alongside the Arnon, which is in the desert extending into Amorite territory. The Arnon is the border of Moab, between Moab and the Amorites.

Deuteronomy 2:24
Set out now and cross the Arnon Gorge. See, I have given into your hand Sihon the Amorite, king of Heshbon, and his country. Begin to take possession of it and engage him in battle.

Deuteronomy 4:47
They took possession of his land and the land of Og king of Bashan, the two Amorite kings east of the Jordan.

Joshua 5:1
Now when all the Amorite kings west of the Jordan and all the Canaanite kings along the coast heard how the Lord had dried up the Jordan before the Israelites until we had crossed over, their hearts melted and they no longer had the courage to face the Israelites.

Joshua 10:6
The Gibeonites then sent word to Joshua in the camp at Gilgal: 'Do not abandon your servants. Come up to us quickly and save us! Help us, because all the Amorite kings from the hill country have joined forces against us.'

Joshua 24:12
I sent the hornet ahead of you, which drove them out before you – also the two Amorite kings. You did not do it with your own sword and bow.

Ezekiel 593–570 Ezekiel 16:3
Say, 'This is what the Sovereign Lord says to Jerusalem: Your ancestry and birth were in the land of the Canaanites; your father was an Amorite and your mother a Hittite.'

Ezekiel 16:45
You are a true daughter of your mother, who despised her husband and her children; and you are a true sister of your sisters, who despised their husbands and their children. Your mother was a Hittite and your father an Amorite.

Amos c.760 Amos 2:9
I destroyed the Amorite before them,
  though he was tall as the cedarsand strong as the oaks.
I destroyed his fruit above and his roots below.

Nebo in the Bible

Numbers 32:3
Ataroth, Dibon, Jazer, Nimrah, Heshbon, Elealeh, Sebam, Nebo and Beon

Numbers 32:38
...as well as Nebo and Baal Meon (these names were changed) and Sibmah.
They gave names to the cities they rebuilt.

1230 Numbers 33:47
They left Almon Diblathaim and camped in the mountains of Abarim, near
Nebo.

Deuteronomy 32:49
Go up into the Abarim Range to Mount Nebo in Moab, across from Jericho, and
view Canaan, the land I am giving the Israelites as their own possession.

Deuteronomy 34:1
Then Moses climbed Mount Nebo from the plains of Moab to the top of Pisgah,
across from Jericho. There the Lord showed him the whole land – from Gilead
to Dan.

1 Chronicles 5:8
And Bela son of Azaz, the son of Shema, the son of Joel. They settled in the area
from Aroer to Nebo and Baal Meon.

Isaiah 742–700 Isaiah 15:2
Dibon goes up to its temple, to its high places to weep;
    Moab wails over Nebo and Medeba.
    Every head is shaved and every beard cut off.

Jeremiah 621–580 Jeremiah 48:1
Concerning Moab:
This is what the Lord Almighty, the God of Israel, says:
'Woe to Nebo, for it will be ruined.
    Kiriathaim will be disgraced and captured;
    the stronghold will be disgraced and shattered.'

Jeremiah 48:22
To Dibon, Nebo and Beth Diblathaim,...